THE
TRIBULATION
PEOPLE

THE TRIBULATION PEOPLE

by

Arthur D. Katterjohn
with Mark Fackler

Creation House
Carol Stream, Illinois

© 1975 by Arthur D. Katterjohn. All rights reserved.
Published by Creation House, 499 Gundersen Drive,
Carol Stream, Illinois 60187
In Canada: Beacon Distributing Ltd., 104 Consumers Drive,
Whitby, Ontario L1N 5T3

Printed in the United States of America
First Printing—October, 1975
Second Printing—February, 1976

ISBN 0-88419-115-x
Library of Congress Catalog Card Number 75-24586

CONTENTS

PREFACE

Jesus is coming again—He said He would!

The return of Jesus Christ will be the climactic event in world history; it is the only hope for our sin-sick society; it is that blessed hope to which all Christians eagerly look. This book is about that return, and its effect on the believers of today—who may well be the tribulation people of tomorrow.

We have designed it to help in your personal Bible study. Keep your Bible open as you read. This book is also for use in adult Sunday School classes with suggested topics for discussion, projects and questions for group interaction at the end of each chapter. There is one for each Sunday in the quarter, a three-month study of eschatology.

I am grateful to the many people who have encouraged me in this project. I am especially indebted to the Rev. Elmer Katterjohn—my father, and a Baptist minister for forty years, under whose preaching I came to know the Lord, to respect the authority of the Word of God, and to love the words of Jesus; and to the Rev. Bob Nelson—the pastor whose question started me on this quest which has taken almost ten years: "Art, are you sure the Bible really teaches what you believe about the rapture? Show me."

I am deeply grateful to my faculty colleagues at Wheaton College who have encouraged me so much, to the students who have been so interested in discovering Bible truth about the rapture, and to the atmosphere of honest debate, serious study, and freedom to speak as led by the Spirit of God that we enjoy on that historic Christian campus, a school dedicated to "Christ and His Kingdom."

Dr. Robert Webber, of the Wheaton College Bible Department, has been particularly encouraging during the writing of this, and Dr. J. Barton Payne, a respected author and colleague, gave invaluable assistance in working the kinks out of the final manuscript.

I am also indebted to the many authors who have written about the rapture in a scholarly way—authors whose books I have eagerly devoured and referred to here. My wife Rosemary deserves particular thanks for her loving encouragement. She has had more than her share of stress because of my "outspokenness" on the rapture question.

It is my prayer that this book will deeply affect your ' commitment to the Lord Jesus Christ and that you will look with renewed eagerness for His return, "Who shall come the second time unto salvation." God bless you.

Arthur Katterjohn

Chapter One

VACATION DOESN'T START
UNTIL YOU GET THERE

A friend once told the story of her father who would load the family into the car every summer and drive relentlessly to their destination despite pleas from the kids to stop for a break. Dad's idea was that vacation doesn't start until you get there.

Jesus expressed the sentiment in a different way when He told His people to watch and work until He returned. Followers too eager for heavenly rest were reminded that the earthly sojourn of the Christian demanded diligent service as well as hopeful expectancy. Promises of rest and reward at the finish line, as well as strength for the race, energized the disciples' efforts for the kingdom. They worked for a Master who regularly reminded His men that the world and its people would give them trouble, but the end of their faith would be joy—the joy of intimate, loving fellowship with the sovereign God of the universe.

A different mood has captured God's people today. It's not escapism, as if the Church were simply marking time. But the tension is gone. Christian service is more soufflé than sacrifice, and fellowship is more frequent over coffee and cookies than tears. We're ready for Satan's little troubles—a flat tire on Sunday School rally day—but the big stuff is part of the past. The Colosseum is a monument to early church martyrdom, a mute reminder of persecution that shall nevermore pursue us. After all, doesn't Scripture somewhere teach that Jesus is coming before the heat turns on?

And so we dream. Popular gospel songs declare the theme of Jesus' surprise reentry, and evangelical films scare children into hasty professions of faith by threatening that some night soon mommy or dad may be snatched away forever into heavenly glory—"I wish we'd all been ready!"

Contrary to the hope of many devout and godly believers, the Bible may suggest that history is on a crash course to the most concentrated and worldwide trouble of all time, with God's people on the center of the burner. Evil men will find easy power as convulsing nations beg for stability and capitulate social ideals to leaders who promise normalcy in exchange for limitless authority. Then one leader will emerge, a man more perverse than history's lowest infidel, demented enough to demand that nations worship him, ruthlessly jealous of any higher thing.

The Christian's call, both then and now, is always to endure, to fight the good fight, to press toward the mark, to keep the faith, to run well. And if the Master's gentle encouragement was meant to sustain Christian vigor during the normal course of history, how much more will His words become strength during the final testing period?

The early rapture of the Church can be a pious wish or a firmly defended doctrinal tenet. The former is understandable from a human point of view—only disturbed men and cross-country runners want to suffer. The latter, however, is a matter for Scripture to decide, and this book has been written for the Christian who wants to take another look at end-times doctrine before committing himself to a course of action, for the content of faith and doctrine must always find expression in action. Does Biblical teaching on the rapture make a difference in a Christian's conduct and life-priorities? Are there things we should do now in light of the Bible's persistent warnings about Antichrist and the final period of worldwide persecution? Does it matter whether one is a spectator to the tribulation or a participant? Should the Church prepare to endure or make ready for an unprecedented and unannounced return of Christ just before the tribulation period?

End-times doctrine can be an intricate maze of pre's, post's and a's, with numerous variables connected with each position. In this study guide, however, only one question will be the focus of our search, and it is the most important question on the end times. Could the Bible teach that Jesus will return at the end of the tribulation, and that believers living before His return will be faced with the most devastating persecution ever endured by the saints of any period? The question gains its serious importance from the possibility that we may be those tribulation people.

At the outset of our study, we need to define the words that describe the options taught about the end times. Basically there are three, and each is held by men of unquestionable Christian commitment.

Postmillennialism teaches that the Kingdom of God is now spreading throughout the world as the Church proclaims the Gospel to every creature. Most of the world's population eventually will accept Christianity, and Christ will return after a long period of righteousness and peace on earth known as the millennium. Advocates of this theory are quick to point out that sin will not be completely eliminated until Christ returns. Nevertheless, the majority of people from every nation will be professing Christians by the time Jesus reappears in person.

Amillennialism foresees the return of Christ at the peak of conflict between the forces of good and evil. While the Church is developing through the extension of the Gospel, unredeemed men will sink into deeper cesspools of violence, pride and evil. Some amillennialists hold to a short, future period of intense persecution called the Great Tribulation. Others feel that the tribulation described in Scripture occurred at the destruction of Jerusalem in A.D. 70, and any Biblical references to a future tribulation are a symbolic way of describing the conflict between the Gospel and evil forces throughout the church age.

Premillennialism claims that Christ will reign on earth during a future period of approximately 1000 years while Satan is detained in the abyss. Until recently, premillennialists believed that Christ would return once—at the conclusion of the Great Tribulation—and that His return would herald the beginning of the millennium. This point of view is called historic premillennialism, since its roots can be traced as far back as the early church fathers. It should be noted that some historic premillennialists believed that Jesus' second coming could occur at any time and that the tribulation could already be in progress. Others felt that the tribulation still lay ahead. But all agreed that Christ's return would terminate the tribulation.

A more recent trend holds that Christ will return twice, and that no further prophetic events must occur before He comes the first time. This return, commonly called the rapture, could happen today or next month. Christian believers will, be suddenly and secretly caught up to heaven before the appearance of Antichrist and the start of tribulation.

What does this latter kind of premillennialism involve? Upon Christ's first return, invisible to the world as a whole, God's people will be taken to heaven, there to appear before the judgment seat of Christ. Rewards will be distributed according to faithfulness, and the marriage of the Lamb will unite the Lord with His Bride, the Church. Following the rapture, the tribulation begins on earth, and God's redemptive program begins to focus on Israel. The Man of Sin, Antichrist, emerges. At the same time, the False Prophet, the silver-tongued accomplice of the world ruler, appears, and those who follow him in the worship of the Beast receive a brand on their forehead or hand. During the tribulation, 144,000 converted Jewish missionaries preach the Gospel of the coming kingdom throughout the world, and many respond to their message. Martyrdom decimates the ranks of believers. Nonetheless, their message is effective, despite the conspicuous absence of the Holy Spirit (His ministry is believed to have ceased with the rapture). Survival, a dismal and unhappy alternative, will demand the lifestyle of an underground fugitive. At the conclusion of the tribulation, Christ will return again, this time visible to all, to meet and destroy the armies of Antichrist near the Mount of Olives in Israel, to judge Antichrist and the False Prophet, to resurrect the tribulation martyrs, and to begin His millennial kingdom in which the glorified Church and restored

Israel will share His reign.

According to many *pre*tribulationists, the rapture is called in Scripture the "Day of Christ" and can happen any time. The rapture, of course, is different from the return or second coming, which happens after the tribulation and is associated with the "Day of the Lord." Church saints are not the same as tribulation saints, who are called in the book of Revelation "elect," "saints" or "Israel." Implicit in this popular chronology is the belief that God deals with different men in different ways at different times. The Gospel preached during the tribulation will be noticeably different from the one we have grown accustomed to during the Church age.

*Post*tribulationists, or historic premillennialists, believe that Scripture mentions only one coming of Christ—at the end of the tribulation. Before that happens, the Gospel of salvation through faith in Christ must be preached to every tongue and nation. The Antichrist will appear and assume the authority of a world monarch not content with temporal power alone, but ambitious to the point of declaring himself an object of worship. Persecution against loyal Christians will be vigorous. The Great Tribulation will levy a heavy toll on all who resist the worship of Antichrist. Then salvation will dawn as a morning star—Christ will return in triumph and glory. The normal posttribulationist (posttribber) is neither a disturbed man nor does he necessarily enjoy cross-country marathons, but his scriptural findings place the Church on earth during the tribulation and define the rapture as an event simultaneous with, and equivalent to, the glorious return.

This book is about the time of the rapture, the most pressing question of the future. The millennial issue, whether a thousand-year reign of Christ on earth separates the now-world from eternity, or whether we are ushered immediately into the new heavens and the new earth, is secondary to the crucial question of the time of Jesus' return. For when He returns, we shall be with Him, and the location of our fellowship is incidental. Sincere men from every Christian heritage lock horns over the millennium debate, failing to see that open fellowship with Christ promises a quality of life that would make any environment shine with joy.

Furthermore, in this book, we will argue that the fact of the return, more than the imminence of the rapture, is our proper motive for Christian conduct and service. Posttribulationists maintain that the Church will endure persecution under Antichrist's anarchy, but will be spared from the wrath of God which falls during the latter part of the tribulation. In contrast to the advocates of early removalism, the posttriber finds no basic distinction between the Church, the elect, the saints, or faithful Israel in God's economy of salvation. All believers, heirs of salvation by grace through faith, are part of the Body of Christ. God's plans and purposes are consistent and unchanging. The Church, the Gospel, the Holy Spirit on earth, worldwide witnessing, and tribulation will all continue until the victorious revelation of Jesus Christ, when He will be seen by all to be King of kings, and Lord of lords.

Why all the fuss about definitions and details? Wrangles over obscure timetables seem out of place in a world writhing in famine, racism, and nuclear anxiety. The future becomes a blur in the frenzy of the present, and the "pantribulationist" offers easy confidence that everything will pan out in the end, anyway.

But hope is the dream of action, and Christians should know what their hope is. Whoever is earnest about discovering the truth of Scripture can never settle for someone else's homework. Bible study takes work, patience and prayer. The Word comes alive as each believer searches it and senses that the teacher, the Holy Spirit, is blending revealed truths to make him a dedicated and capable Christian workman. Determine before the study that every man's argument (including our own) must stand the test of Scripture, then attack this puzzling rapture question with the confidence that God Himself has something He wants you to know concerning it.

This is a handbook for those who seek to understand the return of Christ. It is, at the same time, a Bible study guide and a short commentary on New Testament passages which describe the great hope of all believers. It was written with the conviction that the church is deluged with theories about the

Lord's return, and that preparation for the end times demands a return to scriptural teaching, not fanciful theorizing.

In a recent full-page advertisement in *The New York Times,* the alleged prophet Sun Myung Moon described the imminent return of Christ "as the Son of man in the flesh . . . in the capacity of the Third Adam," who with the Third Eve, will lay "the foundation of the Kingdom of God on earth." Effective propagandists may dissuade the faith of some who are unsure of the prophetic truth of God's Word. Now is not a time for doubt and uncertainty, but for integrated and obedient awareness of God's revealed will.

Despite current popularity of the pretribulation rapture teaching, the Bible may indeed declare that the Church will endure intense tribulation before it sees its Lord. The tribulation, as the name implies, will not be a happy time for God's people. Hunger, economic pressure, imprisonment, death, and worldwide oppression will characterize these final days on earth.

Loyalty to Jesus will face its most strenuous test, and perseverance will require more resolute courage, more brother-helping brotherliness, and more sheer resistance of evil than ever a generation of Christian believers has needed. The Master's comfort will surely be evident to those who go through it, and His requirement of discipleship—"take up your cross daily"—will be the hourly challenge of faithful disciples across the globe.

But before you start stockpiling food in underground bunkers, study the New Testament, digest the total picture of the end times, and determine in prayer to watch and work whatever the cost, and however long the wait.

In his last broadcast before his retirement, Chet Huntley, famed newscaster of the 1960s and early 1970s, encouraged an audience of millions with the promise that "better news is ahead . . . if we will work for it." The Christian has heard a heavenly herald pronounce better news: He is coming! The same spirit of progressive optimism that looks ahead to better days is combined with prophetic reality in the Biblical picture of a Satan-inspired world ruler, Antichrist, who will scourge the earth before the Lion of Judah returns to inaugurate His kingdom of endless, intimate fellowship with His people. Better days are ahead, but first the ominous period of testing and trial when faith in Christ will be a heinous crime, and followers of the Lamb will pay for their loyalty in blood.

Scripture reading

Get acquainted with the main New Testament passages on the return of Christ: Matthew 24, I Corinthians 15, I Thessalonians 4, II Thessalonians 2, and Revelation 19 and 20. You might also note how an Old Testament saint responded to trouble in the short book of Habakkuk, with special attention to chapter three, verses 17-19.

Integration

1. Which would you prefer—to endure the tribulation or be raptured before it all gets started?

2. Examine your background. Which of the end-times arguments are you most familiar with? Have you been taught that the posttribulational view is a *liberal* idea?

3. Can you point to scriptural evidence for a pretribulation rapture? Make sure your evidence states the facts. Indirect references are not enough. List the verses that teach two returns of Christ—one of them secret, invisible and occurring before the tribulation.

4. Are you preparing for trouble, just in case? What attitudes should you develop toward your property, witnessing, and Bible memory? What plans should your church make for worship during the tribulation? How can a Christian tone his spiritual muscle to resist capitulating to Antichrist and remain truly loyal to Jesus?

Chapter Two

FOCUS: TALKS ON THE
MOUNT CALLED OLIVET

Matthew 24-25

As Jesus walked from the temple, leaving behind a squad of stunned and red-faced Pharisees (they weren't accustomed to being called snakes to their faces), the disciples approached Him and began to admire the surrounding architecture, perhaps like we might bashfully speak of the weather to a friend who has just endured a stormy encounter. But the Master turned their pensive chatter into His greatest lesson on prophecy, and His perceptive honesty freed them to question Him on matters that could only be mentioned in private.

"When will these things be, and what will be the sign of Your coming, and the end of the age?" they asked. Let's read and consider precisely what Jesus told them, because He was speaking to us, His Church, His people.

Some claim that Christ was talking only to the Jews in Matthew 24 and 25, and that what He had to say means nothing for Christians today. But these chapters make no mention of Israel or the Jews; in fact, Jesus was speaking intimately with the nucleus of the New Testament Church—the team of missionaries that would proclaim the first Spirit-empowered message to 3,000 converts in Jerusalem, and from there to the distant corners of the known world. Later in the same week, Jesus would give the teachings recorded in John 14-17 to the same group, and no one has ever quarreled about whether John 14:3 refers to the Church. Neither should we question His intended audience in Matthew 24-25. George

Ladd, author of several books on the end times, points out that Old Testament prophecies (for example Joel 2:28-32 and Jeremiah 31:31-34) have their fulfillment both in the Church and in Israel.

> We are on church ground, not Jewish ground in Acts 2 and Hebrews 8 even though the Old Testament predictions appear to be exclusively on Jewish ground. Why are we not also on church ground as well as on Jewish ground in Matthew 24 . . . The assumption that this is exclusively Jewish ground is a human interpretation which is not supported by the Word of God.[1]

Matthew 24:3—Key word

The key word in the Discourse occurs in the disciples' question, and it is the first occasion of the word in Matthew: "What is the sign of the *parousia* and the close of the age" (NASB)? The word *parousia* means arrival and signifies the personal presence of someone who has come. In Greek literature, it was used to describe the arrival of a high dignitary on an official visit. There is no better word to describe the royal arrival of the King of kings. Every time *parousia* is mentioned in the New Testament, it refers to the Lord's coming, and according to 1 Thessalonians 4:15-17, the rapture will take place at the *parousia* of the Lord.[2] If we can determine when the *parousia* happens, we will know at what point in prophecy the rapture will occur.

Matthew 24:4-14—Key task

Jesus warned His men that the Church age would be characterized by deceivers, false prophets, even false christs. War and threats of more war, pestilence, famine and earthquakes would shatter political and ecological balance and signal the approach of His return, "but that is not yet the end." One task must be fulfilled before the close of the age and the return of Christ. The Gospel must be preached throughout the entire world as a witness to all nations, "and then the end shall come" (v. 14). Christ clearly stated that every nation must hear the good news before He comes back.

Now, those who think that Jesus was speaking here only to faithful Israel believe also that the "Gospel of the kingdom" (v. 14) is somehow different from the Gospel we know today. The Gospel of the kingdom, they say, is a unique message that the Jewish evangelists will preach during the tribulation. It has little to do with the Gospel of grace through faith in Jesus Christ. God will institute a different way of salvation for the hard-pressed believers under Antichrist's reign. But if the Bible doesn't make a distinction, can we?

When Jesus preached the Gospel of the kingdom, it was a call to repent and believe (Mark 1:14-15). For Paul, the Gospel of grace and the Gospel of the kingdom were one and the same (Acts 20:24-28; 28:23, 30-31), and he warned against anyone who tried to distort, change, or add to the Gospel of Christ (Galatians 1:7-8). In Revelation, it is the *eternal* Gospel which is preached to every person on earth (Revelation 14:6). To find four different Gospels, as pretribulationists do, is to confuse titles with content. A difference in labels does not necessarily mean a difference in innards.[3]

Matthew 24:15-28—Key event

Here Jesus describes the specific event that will precede His coming. Antichrist must appear. The Abomination of Desolation is Antichrist's desecration of the temple at Jerusalem, when he will proclaim himself God (much like the Roman emperors did during the early Church age) and make war against the saints (II Thessalonians 2:4; Revelation 13:4-8). When Antichrist claims to be God, the countdown of world history has begun.

Two words that seem quite simple are crucial to Jesus' story here. The *when* of verse 15 signals the *then* of verse 21. The word translated "then" is *tote,* and it means "at the same time." In other words, the great tribulation will begin at the same time the Beast climbs the temple steps and plops arrogantly upon the throne. During the tribulation, con-men and agents of the regime will claim that the Lord has come, and point to phony christs like carnival barkers draw crowds into side-shows.

Matthew 24:22, 24—Are you one of the elect?

The "elect" brings up a special word and another fork in the road between pre- and posttribulationists. Throughout the New Testament, we shall see as the study progresses, the elect are God's chosen people, and it is for their sake that He shortens the time of the tribulation. Who are the elect of Romans 8:33, the called of Matthew 22:14, the chosen people of Titus 1:1, Colossians 3:12, and II Timothy 2:10 if not the Church? Likewise in Matthew 24, the elect refers to the Church, those Christians who are alive during Antichrist's incredible climb to power, and who will endure his ill-fated persecutions.

In the account of the Olivet Discourse recorded in the Gospel of Mark, the elect are gathered from the four winds, from every isle and fjord on earth, and also, surprisingly, from heaven (13:27). The dead in Christ will accompany the Lord when He comes and believers alive on earth will join them to receive their resurrection bodies. Parallel passages in I Thessalonians 4:16-17 and I Corinthians 15:50-54 leave no doubt that Jesus and Paul are talking about the same event. It's a great hope—our greatest hope—"therefore comfort one another with these words" (I Thessalonians 4:18).

Matthew 24:29-36—The Lord's return

Have you ever seen a private thunderstorm or a secret lightning bolt? Jesus compared His return to these eruptions of nature (v. 27), and made it clear that when He returns, the world is going to know! Here the word *parousia* appears again, specifically located after the rise of Antichrist and the tribulation, and as we shall presently see, at the same time as the wrath of God.

With electric excitement, Jesus announces the cosmic overture to His royal entrance. A darkened sun, a faceless moon, plummeting stars, and rumbling heavens will signal the end of Antichrist's short but terrible reign and the approach of the One called faithful and true, the Word of God (Revelation 19:11, 13). Nonbelievers will mourn while Christians meet their Lord, and the fig tree's summer leaves (v. 32) will give way to the harvest of resurrection and victory.

Peter describes the same natural eruptions as preceding the great day of the Lord (Acts 2:19-20). John mentions them under the sixth seal (Revelation 6:12-17) which precedes the day of God's wrath, and again in the third and fourth trumpets (Revelation 8:10-12) which come before Jesus' reign at the seventh trumpet; and yet again in the fifth bowl (Revelation 16:10) prior to Christ's revelation as King of kings.

When nature explodes, terror grips the world, and people cringe to see the glory of God descend to claim His earth (Revelation 1:7). Kneeling rebels beg mountains to cover them and rocks to hide them (Revelation 6:16), for the One whose presence they have resisted for so long has returned in anger. What a contrast to believers, who recognize their Lord with intuitive insight, and feel the joy of fulfilled hope surge into their hearts like whitecaps pound the shoreline, for they "shall see Him as He is" (I John 3:2).

Jesus has answered the disciples' question: What will be the sign of your coming? There is no clearer scriptural statement on the time of the Lord's return. Other Bible passages corroborate the message (compare II Thessalonians 1-2 and Revelation 19-20). Every specific Scripture that speaks of a time relationship between the tribulation and the return of Christ places His coming after the tribulation. The coming described in verses 30-31 is the only one Jesus mentions. It is His one-time return to rapture His Church and inaugurate His kingdom.

The parable of the fig tree underlines the main point. The dawning of cosmic signs and wonders will give a period of warning before the sun of history finally sets. No one knows the exact date and hour, and only simpletons are gullible enough to believe "prophets" who claim to know more than Jesus Himself. But the signs are given to strengthen believers in the hope of Jesus' near return. We can be sure that the generation

21

which sees these signs will be the one which welcomes the Lord to earth.

Matthew 24:37-39—The days of Noah

Noah was eccentric. Who else ever built a boat in the middle of a desert? Imagine the jokes that went around local bridge parties and ministerial conferences.

But Noah knew something his contemporaries did not. He knew that God was unhappy and that judgment was coming soon. Three conclusions beg discovery in the Noah account, and directly relate to the Lord's return. First, Noah's rescue was on the same day as God's judgment on the ungodly. Is it too much to believe that Jesus wanted us to learn from Noah's experience—that just as God kept His servant from the contamination of a corrupt world and spared him the punishment of judgment, so God will keep His servants of that future day through the "hour of trial" and preserve us from the force of His wrath?

Second, Noah did not just tend the premises while waiting for God to drown the wicked. He preached, warned, urged, pled, and declared the greatness of God and the severity of dabbling with divine patience. Noah never knew exactly when the rain would fall, but he knew it would be soon because the signs were there. Though times were hard, he stayed loyal to his God and his calling. No grandstand seat for him. He built an ark. No grim reports of "They'll never change, why not let them drown!" Noah was a fighter, and a good example for the Church of the end times. In God's providence, the flood could not occur until the ark was finished. For us, the return cannot occur until The Great Commission is accomplished. Perhaps this is the substance of Peter's advice to "look for and hasten the coming of the day of God" (II Peter 3:12).

Third, Noah knew at one point that he had only one week to go, seven days, before the flood (Genesis 7:4). We also will have a countdown, not as precisely as Noah to be sure, but nonetheless indicative of the approaching return. Revelation speaks of seven trumpets, and Christ returns at the last. So Christians will be informed of the approximate, but not the

22

specific, time of Jesus' appearing. The Church today can rightly remember Noah and strengthen itself. God's ark is on the way.

One additional word about Noah. We have mentioned those who apply Matthew 24-25 to a Jewish remnant, who talk about a different "Gospel of the kingdom," and who think the elect are tribulation believers. They also regard Noah as a symbol of the tribulation saints, and claim that Enoch is the true representative of the Church. (Enoch had the unique experience of never dying, but was caught up to heaven by the call of God.) Enoch, in fact, was translated at least 69 years before Noah was even born (Genesis 5:21-28). Could he illustrate the pretribulation rapture? Both Noah and Enoch walked with God, found grace in the Lord's eyes, and came to inherit righteousness by faith (Hebrews 11:5-7). It is not likely that a case for the pretribulation rapture can be built on Enoch's pre-flood translation.

Matthew 24:40-51—The "sudden snatch"

Jesus describes the separation of the righteous from the unrighteous, His people from Satan's people, in verses 40-41. The word for "taken" is a familiar one in the New Testament, *paralambano*. It is the same word used in John 14:3: "If I go and prepare a place for you, I will come again, and *receive* you to Myself." Most Christians understand both passages to describe the rapture, and indeed they do. But the Matthew passage places the rapture in a time sequence in relation to other events. It will occur at the coming of the Son of Man, after the tribulation.

Verse 42 is not an excuse to quit your job and take to the mountains in white choir gowns. "Watch" is correctly translated "be on the alert" (NASB) and means to be watchful and careful. The "day" of the Lord is after the tribulation, according to Paul (I Thessalonians 5; II Thessalonians 2) and for that day we are commanded to watch. Otherwise, Jesus may surprise us like a thief surprises a drowsy house owner (vs. 43-44). "But you, brethren, are not in darkness, that the day should overtake you like a thief; for you are all sons of light and sons of day" (I Thessalonians 5:4, 5).

The command to watch is described in terms of two slaves in verses 45-51. The "faithful and sensible slave" is happy when his master returns because he is alert and busy. But the cloddish slave has catnapped and gets caught in his pajamas instead of his work jeans. Every Christian must heed the warning. It is a matter of attitude and action.

Some critics place posttribulationists in the same class as the evil slave of verse 48, the one who excused his revelry by claiming that the master would not be returning soon. Hold the phone. Is there a difference between Bible study and drunken folly? Jesus Himself placed His return after the tribulation. True believers always will be watchful, ambitious for God, and ready for His return, even though it is on the other side of the tribulation. Watchfulness coupled with energetic service must characterize the Lord's sensible servant. There are many ponderables in the climax of history, but this much is certain—we are to watch and work until He comes.[4]

Matthew 25—Three parables

Three word pictures are used here to describe the coming of Christ. First, Jesus compares the kingdom of heaven to ten virgins waiting for their bridegroom to come. Five wise virgins have sufficient oil to keep their lamps lit even though the groom tarries. Five flighty women let their oil supply dwindle. At midnight the cry is heard, "Behold, the bridegroom! Come out and meet him!" And five lamps are in an oil crisis. The five wise virgins go out to meet the groom and continue on with him to the marriage celebration.

The bridegroom is Jesus Christ. The Church is His bride (Ephesians 5:25-32). The wise virgins are those who know and follow the Lord, and the foolish ones are those who merely profess to know Him. The marriage supper is another element in the same return that Jesus just finished describing (compare 25:13 with 24:36,42,44). The time of the cry—midnight—is indicative of Christ's coming for His believers at their darkest hour, the time of great tribulation and persecution by Antichrist. The same teaching is found in Revelation 19:6-9

24

where the marriage supper occurs after the tribulation, after Antichrist, and after the announcement of the reign of the Lord God Almighty. The marriage supper is posttribulational.

The second parable relates the sad story of a timid slave who chose to bury his talent instead of to use it. Upon his master's return he was red-faced and empty-handed. When asked why he had not even taken the initiative to place the talent in a bank, the indolent servant could only mumble a feeble excuse and return the original talent, unharmed at least, but also unused. The faithful servants, on the other hand, multiplied the master's investment and were appropriately rewarded for their work.

First, note that the master returned "after a long time" (v. 19). The text does not say that the servants knew his trip would be lengthy, but they must have expected more than a brief excursion. After all, had not the master entrusted them with his estate? Had not he charged them with a commission to multiply his possessions? Could this be done in a day? Likely not, and the clear meaning is that delay must not bring discouragement. The Christian who is alert to Jesus' return must be active about the work the Master has given him. We know He is coming, and we know there is a job to do beforehand.

Second, both rewards and punishments are given when the master returns. Pretribulationists insist that rewards are dispensed at the rapture, while judgment is meted at the return, seven years later. That idea counters Matthew 16:27, where Jesus teaches that every man will be recompensed at His glorious return. Be alert for man-made distinctions where the Word teaches an identity.

The third parable is the most difficult to decipher. Who are the nations, the sheep, the goats? How can nations be judged when the overriding theme of Scripture is salvation through personal rebirth? Has "social action" become the ground for blessing and punishment?

Amid the ponderables, one teaching in this parable rings clear—namely, judgment is posttribulational: "When the Son of Man comes in glory . . . He will sit on His glorious throne" (v.

31). And most Christians believe His "glorious coming" is after the tribulation. The term "sheep" is significant. How often did the Good Shepherd refer to His people as sheep, and to His kingdom as the fold? Yet the sheep are present at His judgment seat. Paul repeats the news that "we must all appear before the judgment seat of Christ" (II Corinthians 5:10). Christians will stand there confident that nothing can snatch them from the Father's hand (John 10:29). The Church will be gathered together after the tribulation, after the Lord's return, and at the judgment seat of Christ will enter eternal life (v. 46).

Pretribulationists claim that this passage refers to the Jewish remnant saying that "brothers of Mine" (v. 40) must be a reference to Israel. The text, however, offers no mention of a Jewish remnant, and no nationality is identified with either the sheep or the goats. The point is that true faith will find expression in loving-kindness and service. James emphasizes the deadness of faith without works. The present passage exposes the hypocrisy of calling Christ Lord when we do not follow in His steps.

Having studied these two chapters, have you found in Jesus' honest answer to the disciples' earnest question any hint of two returns, or two stages in one return, or a rapture distinct from a return, or a secret visitation of the Lord to claim His Church before the tribulation?

In a pamphlet entitled *Tribulation or Rapture—Which?* Oswald J. Smith tells the story of his "first awakening" to the posttribulation view at a time when he fully believed that Christ would rapture the Church before the tribulation. Dr. Smith was preaching a prophetic series during the early 1920s, and had taken his congregation through the teachings in Daniel. But, as he reports,

> No sooner had I started on Matthew 24 than I got into trouble . . . I was in a maze, for I was perplexed . . . If the rapture was to be before the Tribulation, the Lord Jesus Christ would certainly have given some hint of it at least . . . It is unthinkable that He would have spoken so minutely of the Tribulation without stating that the Church would escape. Instead, He

26

purposely led His hearers to the belief that His followers would be in it. Hence, I was staggered, nor could I honestly defend my previous position . . .

That experience led to a long and thorough re-examination, and Dr. Smith concluded: "When I began to search the Scriptures for myself I discovered that there is not a single verse in the Bible that upholds the pretribulation theory, but that the uniform teaching of the Word of God is of a posttribulation rapture."[5]

He is not alone in that discovery.

Footnotes

[1]George Ladd, *The Blessed Hope,* p. 133.

[2]"For this we say to you by the word of the Lord, that we who are alive, and remain until the *parousia* of the Lord . . ."

[3]George Ladd's *The Gospel of the Kingdom* contains an excellent treatment of the various gospels alleged to be connected with the end times.

[4]See Luke 12:35-48 for more details on the two slaves.

[5]Oswald J. Smith, *Tribulation or Rapture—Which?* London: The Sovereign Grace Advent Testimony, n.d., pp. 3-4.

Scripture reading

Matthew 24-25, Mark 13, and Luke 21.

Integration

1. Prayerfully read the Olivet Discourse at least twice. Draw a time-line noting carefully the order of events Jesus describes in answer to the disciples' question. Compare your time chart with others you have seen, and think through any possible revisions of your own.

2. Take another look at that list of verses you compiled at the end of Chapter One. Were any of them part of the Lord's Olivet talk? If so, examine them again. Remember, indirect inferences are not fair game. Note any new verses you have discovered which seem to teach a pretribulation rapture.

3. Take action. Church members should pray for each other, asking the Lord to build the qualities of alertness and

eager service into the very fiber of the Christian community. Don't hesitate to ask forgiveness if Christ's description of the evil slave (Matthew 24:48; 25:26) hits home.

4. Put yourself in the disciples' place. If you had asked their question, would you be worried at Jesus' answer? Anxious? Distraught? More dependent on Him for strength? More determined in your loyalty to Him?

Chapter Three

WIDE ANGLE:
THE TEACHINGS OF JESUS

In the Gospels

If Jesus had said no more about His coming than the truths of the Olivet Discourse, we would have been suitably equipped to face the most stringent tests of faith with confident thanks to God, "who always leads us in His triumph in Christ" (II Corinthians 2:14). At Olivet, Jesus made His return a most certain article of faith, not merely a wishful hope, but a "yes-promise" upon which His followers could reverently depend.[6] To other instances when Jesus taught prophetic truth we now turn with the same assurance and trust.

Matthew 13:24-30, 36-43—The wheat and the tares
Two kinds of people are described in this parable, and each by a plant. Wheat represents Christians, children of light, those who have been redeemed. Tares, which were a tough field weed called darnel, picture the devil's counterfeit—quasi-religious pretenders who associate with the Church and perhaps even give support to a diluted brand of Christianity, but who actually are children of the world and the wicked one.

Both groups, we learn, are to continue intermingled until the time of harvest. Both true believers and false intruders, Christians and charlatans, possessors and professors, are to coexist in public Christendom until the "end of the age" (v. 39).

A problem arises about which "age" Jesus is referring to.

29

Various explanations, some intelligible and others bizarre, have been offered. The plain meaning of the phrase, both here and throughout the New Testament, is that span of time between Christ's two visible breakthroughs into history. We are in that age now. And the harvest—the separation of the weeds from the wheat—brings to a close this present age.[7]

The harvest is accomplished by angels acting under command of Christ (Matthew 24:31, Revelation 14:14-20). The reapers are told to "gather out" all the imposters and throw them into flames fanned by the anger of God against those who falsely claim to be His children. By contrast, the "gathering together" of the wheat into the kingdom of their Father is identical to the gathering of the elect in Matthew 24:31 at the coming of the Lord. It is the resurrection of the righteous spoken of in Daniel 12:2-3: "And many of those who sleep . . . will awake . . . and those who have insight will shine brightly like the brightness of the expanse of heaven."

The story, then, pictures Christendom during our present age as comprised of two strains—genuine disciples and phony religious pretenders. Both are destined for the harvest; first the tares, then the wheat. There is no mention of tares remaining on earth after wheat has been raptured; there is no inkling that a seven-year tribulation separates two phases of the harvest. Both tares and wheat coexist until the event which culminates the age—the return of Christ. At the harvest, one group shines forth, the other gnashes teeth. Though tares may be tough, wheaties are the real champions.

Matthew 13:47-52—The dragnet

In His last of seven parables in this section, Christ gives to His disciples another picture of His kingdom in the present age. A great net is cast into the sea, comes up full of fish, and the good catch is separated from the bad.

No new information is given in this parable, but it corroborates truths earlier expressed. The righteous and the wicked in Christendom exist together until the consummation of the age. When the good is gathered, the bad is cast away—a unified event that suggests a simultaneous rescue of the redeemed and judgment of the damned. No time interval between the catches, and no early removal of the good fish, are mentioned. Both "delectable" and "rough" are together until the end, when for the wicked, the proverbial frying pan will take on literal truth.

Matthew 16:17-28—The Church and its reward

It was characteristic of Jesus to introduce important truths to His disciples in chewable, tidbit portions. Gradually, as the men became aware of the import and meaning of His teachings, Jesus would develop, expand and refine doctrines and life-attitudes that had been introduced on earlier occasions. As a teacher, Jesus never intended to complete His curriculum. Even at the end, He promised the coming of the Spirit who would guide them into "all the truth" (John 16:13).

So it is not unusual that Jesus would introduce truths in this chapter of Scripture that are picked up later on. He gives Peter a morsel of redemptive truth in verse 17, and a taste of Church truth in verses 18-19. He tells them the bare facts of His crucifixion and resurrection in verses 21-23, and turns their aggressive reaction into a lesson on life priorities in verses 24-26. Then, immediately following His instruction that discipleship includes a willingness to bear the cross even to death, He tells the twelve about His second coming, and assures them that every man will be recompensed at that time according to his deeds.

At what time? When the Son of man comes in the glory of His Father with His angels. And when is that? Jesus pinpointed the time in the Olivet Discourse—"immediately after the tribulation . . . they will see the Son of man coming on the clouds of the sky with power and great glory. And He will send forth His angels . . ." (Matthew 24:29-31).

Jesus teaches only one time of reward for all believers. There is no hint of two rewards, given at two times, one before the tribulation and one after. Only one time of recompense is taught, and only one coming. Compare this passage with Revelation 22:12 where Christ promises to reward every man according to his deeds at His "quick coming."

The unity and wholeness of the time of rewards is supported by the next verse, an initial puzzler in which Jesus promises that certain of His disciples will not die until "they see the Son of man coming in His kingdom." This is an allusion to the transfiguration, where Jesus appears in glory and majesty with Moses, who may represent all the believers who have died and are resurrected into the kingdom, and Elijah, who may portray those who do not see death, but are translated directly into the kingdom, namely those believers who are alive at Jesus' coming.

Matthew 28:16-20—The Great Commission

It was not characteristic of Jesus to permit idleness and encourage phlegmatic inactivity. No doubt the remaining eleven felt quite overwhelmed on the mountain the day Jesus gave His final command to make disciples of all nations. But sufficient power came forty days later, and the giant task of worldwide evangelization began.

How long was the Church instructed to continue in its sacrifice and service so that the world's people could hear of redemption in Christ? Jesus' final words give the answer: "Even to the end of the age." It is the same word *end (suntelia)* that we encountered in the parable of the wheat and tares. It refers to the point in history when Jesus returns in glory.

Christians have a job to do, a task that must be done before the Lord returns. Early removal is not our hope. The return of Christ is.

> Christ is tarrying until the Church has completed its task. The world is nearly evangelized: any generation which is really dedicated to the task can complete the mission. The Lord can come in our own generation, in our lifetime, if we stir ourselves to finish the task.[8]

Luke 17:26-37—The days of Noah

"As it was in the days of Noah, so shall it be also in the days of the Son of man" (Luke 17:26). Much of this important

32

passage already has been discussed in our chapter on the Olivet Discourse, but some points brought out by Luke warrant further emphasis.

Normal activities during the days of Noah are the same ones we experience today—eating, drinking and marrying. All of these continued "until the day Noah entered into the ark," when "the flood came and destroyed them all." Both God's rescue of His people and judgment on the wicked happened in quick succession. The time interval between Noah's entering the ark and the first signs of flooding was short indeed. In fact, Genesis 7:7 states that Noah went into the ark "because of (or driven by) the waters of the flood." We can expect therefore that the coming of Christ and the judgment on wickedness will occur in almost spontaneous succession.

Likewise, people pursued their regular daily activities during the "days of Lot" (v. 28). But on the same day that Lot hiked out of Sodom, fire and sulphur rained from the sky and devastated the city. On the same day that God delivers His people, judgment will fall on the wicked.

Since the same day brings both rapture and wrath, the question arises: "What is the order? Will believers be raptured before God pours out wrath, or must Christians also endure this final, worldwide judgment?

It is extremely important to understand that saints will never suffer the wrath of God. Christ Himself suffered in our place and tasted death for us that we should live forever (Hebrews 2:9). "We are not appointed unto wrath, but to salvation" (I Thessalonians 5:9). Noah was first shut in the ark, then the flood waters fell. When Christ comes at the close of the age, He will first gather the saints to Himself, then dispense the judgment of God on the wicked. Matthew's account gives the same order—first the coming of Christ for the elect (Matthew 24:30-32), then the judgment (Matthew 25:31-46). First rapture, then wrath.

Verse 30 speaks of the "day when the Son of man shall be *revealed*" and uses the verb form of the Greek noun *apokalupsis,* or revelation. Clearly then, this must be the posttribulational unveiling of Christ as King (Revelation

33

19:16). But note well the parallel verse in Matthew 24:39: "So shall also the coming—*parousia*—of the Son of man be!" Here is the identification of the two terms *apokalupsis* and *parousia* in parallel accounts of the same sermon. The rapture, which occurs at the *parousia* (1 Thessalonians 4:15-17), happens also at the *apokalupsis,* for these are the same event. Rapture and revelation occur as a single event at the same point in time, just before the wrath of God falls on unrepentant and rebellious planet earth.

Luke 19:11-27—The imminent kingdom

One day on the road to Jerusalem, the disciples approached Jesus with the misconception that the kingdom was to immediately appear, and the Teacher knew once again that He had to set the record straight, to bind up the frazzled edges of the disciples' thin understanding. He told them a parable of the nobleman who gave each of his ten servants a mina (worth about twenty U.S. dollars before inflation) with instructions to multiply it while he was away. The results were tragic for the servants who were Johnny-Go-Do-Nothings, but those who obeyed were blessed.

The disciples knew from Old Testament Scripture (Zechariah 9:9) that the promised Messiah would ride into Jerusalem as a triumphant king, and they wondered if the occasion for which Israel longed had come. No, came Jesus' reply, first He would return to Heaven, assign tasks for His servants to fulfill, then come again with rewards for faithfulness. Their misconception that the kingdom was imminent was quickly dispelled.

The attitude of the waiting servants in this parable is important, for they are instructed not merely to watch and wait, but also to work—making efficient use of the gifts given to the Church (1 Corinthians 12, Ephesians 4), and zealously building disciples of people from all nations (Matthew 28:20). Christ foresaw an entire age, almost two millennia long, of His Church working as the channel of redemptive truth to the world. Only when that "whole earth" task is complete can we legitimately and Biblically expect the Master of the kingdom to return. Whether our ministry is to the primitive aborigine of inland Australia, the sophisticated humanist of Europe, or our neighbor across the street, our job and the message is always the same—tell them of forgiveness and freedom in Christ, trust the Spirit to crack their deadened hearts with the winsome words of God's truth, and nurture into discipleship those who respond. Such is the meaning of Jesus' command, "Occupy till I come."

John 6:22-59—The resurrection
  The Apostle John records more extensively than any other gospel writer Christ's teaching concerning the resurrection. In chapter 5, the Son of man speaks of His own return, "The hour is coming in which all that are in the graves shall hear his voice, and shall come forth; they that have done good, unto the resurrection of life; and they that have done evil, unto the resurrection of damnation" (5:28,29). Christ was teaching that all people would be resurrected, the good and the bad, in two separate resurrections, one unto life and the other unto death.
  In the sixth chapter, Christ gives the time of the resurrection of the righteous. The phrase—"And I will raise him up at the last day"—appears three times, in verses 40, 44 and 54. A similar phrase—"and I should raise it up again at the last day" —occurs in verse 39. There seems little doubt that the resurrection of the righteous will be *at the last day!*
  And when is that? The age before the *parousia* of the Lord (the one in which we are living) is described in Scripture as "this age," "this time," "the time that now is," "the age that now is" and "this present age." Also notice phrases which describe the age to come, the age after the Lord's *parousia:* "that age," "the coming age," "the future age" and "the age which is to come."[9] Since there are only two "ages" in Scripture—*this* age and *that* age—the last day must be that day which brings the present age to a close and opens the door to the age to come.
  No believer will be left in the wake of this awesome resurrection. Jesus promised, "Of all which He hath given me I

should lose none, but should raise it up again at the last day" (v. 39); "every one which sees the Son and believes on Him . . . I will raise him up at the last day" (v. 40); and "whoso eats my flesh and drinks my blood has eternal life, and I will raise him up at the last day" (v. 54). In each case, it is the totality of believers who are included—all the Old Testament people of God, all the New Testament Body of Christ, the Church, which includes (may we say) all the tribulation saints. Christ will leave none of His fellow-heirs behind.

Since all the righteous are to be raised at the last day, we can make important progress in our determination of the time of the resurrection, and thus of the rapture. First, no evidence suggests that some of the righteous are to be raised at a rapture before the tribulation. Also, there is no evidence that the time of the resurrection will be any other than at the last day. All who have the Spirit of God as the pledge and first installment of eternal life (II Corinthians 1:22) may approach death in the radiant prospect of life everlasting. And we who live on are wise not to expect the return of the Lord before that final day!

John 14:1-6—"I will come again!"

In some of the most poetic and oft-memorized verses in the Bible, Jesus tells His disciples that He must go to prepare a place for them, but will come again and receive them unto Himself.

Perhaps more than any other Scripture, this passage has been used to describe the certainty and beauty of Jesus' return. But it also has been abused to say more than it really does. Pretribulation scholars have asserted that John 14:3 is the first hint in Christ's teachings that His return will be in two stages, the first stage before the tribulation. For them, the Lord's words in the Upper Room Discourse constitute a "new revelation," that of another coming distinct from the posttribulational return mentioned earlier in the Olivet Discourse (Matthew 24).

It should not be necessary to defend the integrity and consistency of Jesus' teachings from one part of Scripture to another. We would rather enjoy the purity of the Lord's comforting words given to the eleven remaining disciples on the eve of His crucifixion. Yet we must ask if this "new revelation" hypothesis has substance, if Jesus is introducing a new concept, heretofore undisclosed, as He passes the bread and wine around that intimate chamber.

It already has been mentioned that Jesus gave the Olivet Discourse just two days prior to the teachings of John 14. This is clear from Matthew 26:1-2: "And it came to pass, when Jesus had finished all these sayings (the Olivet Discourse of the preceding chapter), he said unto his disciples, Ye know that after two days is the feast of the passover, and the Son of man is betrayed to be crucified." Both discourses were given to the same disciples during the same week, with an interval of only two days in between. Pretribulationists stand on shaky ground when they say the former was delivered to the Jewish remnant and the latter to the Church.

Phraseology is essentially the same in both sermons. As Jesus begins the Upper Room Discourse in John 13:31, He calls Himself the Son of man, as He does ten times throughout the fourth Gospel. It is the same title used nineteen times in Matthew (three occurrences are in the Olivet Discourse), four times in Mark, and eleven times in Luke—a certain strain of identity. In John 14:3 and Matthew 24:30, Jesus used the phrases "coming" and "coming again," both from the same Greek root *erchomai*, meaning "to come." Is Jesus referring to the same coming in both instances? Nothing indicates otherwise. Moreover, Christ said that He would "receive" His disciples unto Himself. The word for "receive" is identical to that for "taken" in Matthew 24:40-41, where "one shall be taken and the other left." Since the same word *paralambano* is used in both passages, where is the evidence for two separate returns? It dissolves in the coherent identity of Jesus' teachings.

We suggest that the coming of John 14 and the return in Matthew 24 are the same event, and that the essential truth of the rapture and hope of the Christian is contained in the dramatic promise: "Where I am, there you may be also." Whether that involves a thousand-year reign of Christ on earth or the inauguration of His heavenly kingdom, we will be with Him. The spirit of man could ask no more, and find satisfaction in nothing less. That promise alone frees us to live.

Footnotes

6"For as many as be the promises of God, in Him they are yes; wherefore also by Him is our Amen to the glory of God through us" (II Corinthians 1:20).

7The meaning of the word "end" in verses 39, 40, and 49 is important to the timing of the rapture. If *suntelia,* translated consummation, is taken to mean the close, the end point, the completion of a thing, then the end referred to here is clearly the return of the Lord. Some have argued that "end" means final period, or completion of a goal rather than arrival of a point in time. While the debate goes on, suffice it that of the two forms of the Greek word meaning "end," *suntelia* usually refers to a more precise and explicit terminus than its root, *telos.*

8George E. Ladd, *The Blessed Hope,* p. 148.

9For an expanded treatment of these phrases, see Alexander Reese, *The Approaching Advent of Christ,* p. 54.

Scripture reading

Matthew 13:24-52, 16:17-28, 28:16-20; Luke 17:26-37, 19:11-27; John 6:22-59, 14:1-6.

Integration

1. Each of the Bible passages in this chapter has a central theme—an overriding piece of information or instruction by which God wants us to live. Determine the central truth for each of the passages and use it as a basis for prayer, one each day for seven days.

2. Certain themes recur throughout these Bible portions, and well they should since we are concentrating on the time of the rapture. Make a note of the number of times the following themes are mentioned in the passages under study:

The promise of reward to faithful believers_____.

Jesus' return to earth will be in great glory_____.

The Church has a task to perform during the waiting period. _____

Religious hypocrites are doomed_____.

Christians will be resurrected, just as Jesus was_____.

Jesus' return is in two stages, one before the tribulation, the other after_____.

3. Determine if your local Christian fellowship is living in awareness of the Church's blessed hope, the coming of the Lord. What are the implications of these Bible passages for evangelism, attitudes toward personal property (what you give your money to), time-priorities (what you give yourself to), and preparedness for the future.

4. Discuss any other Bible passages in the Gospels relevant to the time of the rapture. Attempt to put together a picture of the end times from the teachings of Jesus.

Chapter Four

FOCUS:
THE TEACHINGS OF PAUL

In the Thessalonian Epistles

Excitement over the possibility of the Lord's imminent return is not the exclusive property of post-World War II fundamentalism. The Church at Thessalonica had its share of end-times enthusiasm, and some believers there even thought the Lord was already on His way. Perhaps that is why Paul's two letters to the Thessalonians are so full of instruction on the rapture, the resurrection, and the return. Nowhere else in the New Testament epistles is so much explained about the end times in so few chapters. In these books, pretribulationists find their strongest proof-texts for a two-stage return and early removal of the Church. Posttribulationists, far from taking a merely defensive posture, are in wholehearted agreement with the Apostles' teachings and are confident that a precise understanding of these verses will lead to a belief in one, and only one, return of the Lord following the tribulation. Now search it out and decide for yourself!

1 Thessalonians 1:1-4—Church, brethren, elect
As a brief introduction, we should note that Paul addressed his letter to the Church, and called fellow believers "brethren," "elect" and, later, "saints" (3:13). Much has been said by early-removal advocates concerning the uniqueness of the term "Church" as an identifying mark of God's people from

40

Pentecost to the rapture. This peculiarity becomes a major issue in the book of Revelation, but keep in mind that Paul uses the terms interchangeably here. All believers are the elect, the brethren, the saints, and the Church. The unity of all men of faith is one of the cornerstones of Christian doctrine and cannot be jettisoned for the sake of an end-times theory. Let's keep the brotherhood together as much as possible—there's enough "segregationism" around without needlessly reading it into the Word.

I Thessalonians 1:10—Waiting for the Son
Christians today, like believers throughout the ages, are waiting for Christ to return. God has set the world's timepiece, and Christ's delay should cause neither discouragement nor doubt. Waiting involves "patience of hope" (v. 3), and confidence that God's deliverance from wrath is certain to come. No believer will ever suffer the wrath of God, but this promise does not guarantee a pretribulation rapture. The tribulation, it must be remembered, is not the wrath of God, but the persecution of the faithful, both Jews and Gentiles, by Antichrist. God's wrath will not be poured out until Christ comes, when Christians are caught up to meet Him in the air.

I Thessalonians 2:19—Joy at His Coming
How many notables have claimed to be the "happiest man alive"? Paul anticipates great joy when, at the Lord's return, his brothers in Christ will stand with him before the King. Truly happy men will be there! The word "coming" in this verse is *parousia,* and we have already learned that Christ pinpointed His *parousia* after the tribulation.

I Thessalonians 3:13—Coming with all His saints
Two small words are vitally important here: *with* and *all.* The first reverses a phrase found in many prophetic books and songs, for we find that Christ is coming primarily *with* His saints, not just *for* His saints. In fact, there is no verse in the Bible which describes the Lord's coming in terms of "for the

41

saints," or "for the Church." But when Christ comes *with* the saints then will He "establish our hearts unblameable in holiness before God."

Christ is coming with *all* His saints—the faithful believers of the Old Testament, the Church age, and the tribulation martyrs—all will be present and participate in this reverent moment of reunion. Are distinctions within the ranks of believers real or fanciful? *All* are included here.

I Thessalonians 4:13-18—The great rapture passage

Religious groups frequently get into trouble when they find more in Scripture than is actually there, and turn either to unBiblical legalism or to the strange doctrinal confusions which characterize popular cults. So let us initially observe that there is no reference to the tribulation in this rapture passage, nor to a secret, any-moment, coming of the Lord, nor to our return to heaven after the rapture. Nor is there any phrase which teaches that the air is the terminus of our journey. Paul's topic is "them which are asleep," and their relationship to believers who are alive at the coming of the Lord. We will examine each verse to discover the truth of this "rapture" passage, so named for the word "caught up" in verse 17, the only time that word occurs in the Bible.

Evidently, as verse 13 indicates, questions had arisen in the Church as to the status of departed saints, and Paul explains that worldly sorrow is unnecessary—there is hope!

In verse 14, Paul still is talking about the coming of the Lord *with* His saints. There has been no change of subject. Verse 15 assures the Church that those who are alive at the Lord's return shall not precede—the old English word is prevent—those who have died in faith. The saints who have fallen asleep are not relegated to a subordinate status at the coming of Christ, but share a prominent part of the event. The article "the" as in "the coming of the Lord," generally points to a singular occurrence or object. For example, should you introduce *the* wife of your pastor at the dedication of the new educational wing, no one would lift a brow. But try introducing *a* wife of the pastor and notice how genteel society responds. The article here calls attention to a singular coming of the Lord.

The word "remain" occurs only two times in Scripture, here and in verse 17, and carries the meaning "to survive." Certain Bible translations actually use "survive" and others come closer to that meaning than the King James word "remain" implies. To survive certainly suggests the endurance of extreme hardship, and this easily coincides with our knowledge of the tribulation, when many will suffer martyrdom at the hands of Antichrist, but some will survive until the coming of the Lord.

Again the word *parousia* is used to describe the Lord's coming in verse 15. Those who await an early rapture almost always presume this "coming" to be pretribulational, forcing themselves into the contradiction of taking the *parousia* of Matthew 24 as a reference to the posttribulation coming, and the *parousia* of I Thessalonians 4 as a reference to the pretribulation coming. Funny games are sometimes played with the language of Scripture. As we examine the following verses, it should become clear that Paul is simply relaying what Jesus taught before, and that the Olivet Discourse and the Thessalonian epistles speak of the same coming—the same *parousia*.

Verses 16-17 describe the specific events of the rapture of the saints and the revelation of Christ. First notice that the Lord will descend. Early removal advocates traditionally distinguish the day of Christ from the day of the Lord. The former, they say, is the rapture, and the latter is the return following the tribulation, although scriptural evidence for this distinction is altogether absent. By their own admission then, this famous rapture passage must describe the posttribulational return, since it is clearly the Lord, the sovereign God, who is returning here.

Ingmar Bergman, the renowned Swedish film producer, has said that God is silent, and that life would be an absurd joke but for redeeming human love. Without detracting in any way from the magnificence of inter-personal devotion, Christians know that God is not silent—that we serve a living God whose passion-filled voice is unmistakably heard as the Spirit proclaims the truth of the Bible to us, and who will be heard again on that climactic day when He returns "with a shout, with the voice of the archangel, and with the trump of God." The shout of God has been appropriately translated "war cry," "cry of command," "charge" and "shout of command to the troops." This is the voice of the Commander-in-chief of the heavenly armies as He unsheathes His sword of right (Revelation 19:11-20).

The archangel's utterance is reminiscent of Daniel 12, where Michael prophesies a "time of trouble such as never was," and conveys Jehovah's promise that deliverance will come "at that time." Christ speaks of sending His angels to gather together His elect at that time of trouble (Matthew 24). The voice of the angel always is associated with the victorious *parousia* of the Lord when He comes with His angelic armies to destroy Antichrist and gather His people. The modern attempt to separate the gathering of the saints from the coming in power and glory stumbles clumsily over these Thessalonian verses. Far from suggesting a time lapse, Paul corroborates the words of the Lord recorded in the Olivet Discourse (Matthew 24:30-31) that the ingathering of the saints will be accompanied by angelic brass.

The "trump of God" (v. 16) is not a fickle kazoo beamed at church-age saints to alert them to a secret rapture, so faint that its frequency escapes the ears of mockers and rebels. The trump is a noise, a blast, a fearful booming fanfare to the arrival of the King of love and judgment. It is the "last trump" mentioned by Paul in I Corinthians 15:42, the "great sound of a trumpet" prophesied by Christ in Matthew 24:31, and the final trumpet of the seventh angel in Revelation 11:15. Trumpets herald the triumphal procession of a person of high office; the trump can announce nothing other than the *parousia* of the Lord.

When the sky peals its thunderous chorus, then "the dead in Christ shall rise first, and we which are alive and remain shall be caught up together with them in the clouds, to meet the Lord in the air." The rapture word, *caught up,* is used here in connection with the resurrection of the dead in Christ and the coming of the Lord. Other occurrences of words which describe the same event (II Thessalonians 2:1, John 14:3,

Matthew 24:31), cement that connection with the glue of divine proclamation. But nowhere does the meaning, usage, or context of the word suggest those distinctives that have become the pretribulation rapture teaching—secrecy, an any-moment coming, a phase-one return prior to the tribulation. These additives may mix well together in the same sauce, but is the recipe taken from Scripture or from popular prophetic newsletters?

Another pretribulation distinctive is associated with the word "meet." It teaches that when we have met the Lord in the air, He will reverse direction, lead us back to heaven, and there we will pass the seven-year period in which tribulation racks the earth. Does the word "meet" mean to change direction and return along the path just traveled? It is used only three times in Scripture: Matthew 25:6, Acts 28:15, and here.

In the first instance, Jesus uses the word to describe the meeting of the five virgins and the bridegroom in the parable we already have discussed. Notice that the bridegroom comes, meets the virgins, and continues on to the wedding feast. He does not change direction; his destination is forward and so he proceeds. The meeting is called "the hour wherein the Son of man comes," joining this parable with the second coming and the consummation of the age.

In Acts 28, the second instance, Paul is traveling toward Rome. Christian brothers were alerted to his arrival, and came as far as the Three Taverns to meet him. From that point, the delegation accompanied Paul to the Imperial city, much encouraged by the exchange of fellowship. Paul approaches, is met, and continues on.

If the word "meet" in I Thessalonians 4:17 has essentially the same meaning as in the other two occurrences, then we get a picture of Christ descending to the earth, being met by His people in the air, and continuing down to set right the heresies of the tribulation. The saints, and not Christ, reverse direction. The Captain of the hosts does not retreat on His way to victory. He continues on.

"And so shall we ever be with the Lord" reminds us that the key to our understanding the end times is *being with Jesus.*

Arguments over an intermediate thousand-year kingdom, and counter-arguments by a-mill and postmillennarians are worthy subjects for study, but will likely not be resolved until history becomes theology's proof. Nevertheless, the promise of fellowship with Christ upon His return is universal, whatever the geographical and political setting. And that, we submit, should be the focus of Christian hope and the tenpenny nail of orthodoxy.

I Thessalonians 5:1-10—Children of the day
One of the frequent themes dramatized by advocates of pretribulationism is the momentary surprise, the sudden shock of the rapture event. Just as a thief in the night darts from the alleyway and startles an unsuspecting pedestrian, so the coming of Christ for His Church will be unannounced and joyously (frightfully?) sudden, they say.

But who will be surprised? Who will be jolted? Not the Christian believer who has given heed to Jesus' words in Matthew 24; not the obedient servant found doing the Master's business upon His return; not children of light; not children of the day. The Thessalonian churchmen were so aware, in fact, of the signs which would precede and foretell the Lord's coming that Paul merely alludes to them, not counting it necessary to repeat the obvious (v. 1). Certainly the Lord will come with the unexpected haste of a thief in the night, but Christians do not walk the streets after dark! Christians walk in light.

False security lulls an unsuspecting world into a mirage of its own making. Business-as-usual becomes the standard routine, and maintenance of the status quo appears to be an unchallenged assumption of godless society—then the Lord returns (v. 3). Professional men, politicians, blue collar workers, cattlemen, young mothers—all who have not sought Him before—run from Him now in vain. Ever thought of sharing that truth at the next Chamber of Commerce social?

Sobriety (single-mindedness), faith, love, and the hope of salvation guard us who are of the day (v. 8), and keep us unto the day of our deliverance. Verse 9 confirms the promise of 1:10—no believer will suffer the wrath of God; all believers

46

will be "caught up" as Christ and His armies descend to do God's righteous thing on earth.

Verse 10 reminds us again of our tenpenny nail, and beautifully capsulizes the message of the Gospel—Christ died, that whether we live or sleep, we will someday live together with Him.

II Thessalonians 1:4-12—The Church's rest from persecution
It is ever the lot of Christian believers to suffer for their faith. Most Western Christians are fortunate (or are they?) in that the general call to suffering has been relatively painless for present generations. We fail to understand that our reprieve is a historical oddity; we mistakenly assume that past generations have done all the suffering necessary as groundwork for our cultured Christian society, and that the way is clear for a gentle ride into glory.

Indeed, we are in a reprieve. Rather than inducing indolence, it should inspire us to channel energies for the proclamation of the Gospel, at the same time keeping mentally alert for an inevitable resumption of persecution. The Thessalonians suffered, but with the assurance that "when Jesus shall be revealed from heaven with His mighty angels," their faith would be vindicated.

In verse 4, Paul commends the Church for their patience and faith amid persecutions and tribulations. The church at Thessalonica was a suffering church. But God permits moral wrongness only for a time, and promises to avenge the wrong when He asserts His rightful rule at the appearing of Christ. God will judge; He will give tribulation to the "tribulaters" (v. 6) and grant rest from persecution to the Church of God. When? At the appearing *(apokalupsis)* of Jesus Christ (v.7). Rapture and wrath rise and fall on the same day, the day of Christ's glorious appearing. Notice again the accompaniment of angels and the certainty of judgment at the return of Christ— at the same return of Christ—at the same return in which the Church is saved.

47

II Thessalonians 2:1-12—The parousia of the Lord

Now Paul turns his attention directly to the great theme that occupies his pen throughout so much of the Thessalonian correspondence, the rapture of the Church. Verse one announces it, and the second chapter explains it.

Paul was perhaps the most outspoken pastor that any flabby Christian could ever hope to avoid. Always ready with a good word of encouragement, Paul could call sin sin in terms that left few shadows of gray. He speaks pointedly here to the misconception current among the Thessalonians that the end was near, insisting that two signs must color the horizon before the day of Christ could dawn—the falling away of the Church, and the rise of the man of sin.

The word used to describe the "falling away" is a familiar one, a transliteration from the original Greek, *apostasy.* (It's even included as an alternate rendering in the margin of a certain annotated Reference Bible.) Apostasy is a rebellion against God and a refusal to submit to holy truth. Though departure from the faith has been a fact of church life ever since the beginning, we have here a clear reference to that final world Christendom which will foolishly negotiate a strained coexistence with Antichrist, only to be swallowed by his treachery in the end.[10]

The second sign is the revelation of the man of sin, a savior-figure who will oppose God, exalt himself as though he were God, and demand worship due only to God. He is a person yet unknown, although history has had its share of precursors, and contemporary events offer little guarantee against the swift rise of such a man. In verse 8 we learn that Antichrist will be revealed as the Wicked One, but not to unbelievers or the apostate church. To them he will appear as a man of peace, a covenant-maker, a messiah. His peace will be treachery, his covenant a mockery, and his messiahship a sham. If the Church is raptured before he appears, as early-removal advocates insist, to whom could Antichrist be revealed as wicked? Only the Church will recognize his true colors; only Christians will know him for who he is. When the Man of sin proclaims himself to be God from the temple of God (an actual building in Jerusalem when Paul wrote this letter in A.D. 58), believers will know that the countdown of history has begun. Watch for newspapers to announce the rebuilding of the Jerusalem temple. That construction will be like building a stage for a dramatic tragedy, worse by far because the actors will not be acting. Antichrist will ascend the temple steps to announce a New Order, a society governed by a man who claims there is none higher. Christians will be his prey.

Verses 6-7 are crucial to our study, since only here is something (the rapture?) explicitly placed before the Man of sin. Pretribulationists find here a reference to the removal of the Church and the Holy Spirit before the rise of Antichrist. If their connection between "restrainer" and Holy-Spirit-in-the-Church is correct, pretribulationism also is correct, since the Church certainly cannot live without the Holy Spirit.

The connection, however, is problematic. Paul did not mention the Holy Spirit or the Church, but assumed that the Thessalonians knew whom (or Whom) he was talking about. In the first chapter of Job, God is the *restrainer,* building a hedge around His servant to fence out Satan. In Revelation 20, an angel *restrains* Satan in the bottomless abyss, forcing the serpent into a prolonged sabbatical. Some scholars have suggested that civil government is the *restrainer,* and this fits well in the context of Paul's writings. The laws of Rome, however fatally disregarded by her own citizenry, were the crossbeams of civilization during Paul's time. And today, should lawlessness erupt worldwide, who would hesitate to welcome even totalitarianism as a solution?

Of greater import to the resolution of our problem here is the precise wording of the final clause of verse 7. Early-removal advocates have tagged the phrase "taken out of the way" as a sure sign that the Church as the Holy Spirit's channel of restraint will be removed before Antichrist appears. The literal meaning of the phrase, however, is "becomes, or arises, out of the midst." Two evangelical scholars have suggested a couple renderings, neither of which necessarily to a pretribulational conclusion.[11]

The first interpretation takes the phrase "arises out of the midst" to mean "coming on the scene" rather than elimination from the scene, and finds there a reference to Antichrist rising out of the middle of the world when God, the restrainer, finally permits his appearance. Two Greek words are used here: *genetai,* which means to come into being, to arise, as in the phrase "there arose a great storm" (hence our word genesis), and *mesou,* from which we get our word "midst." Verse 7 would then read: " . . . only he (God) who now restrains will do so until he (Antichrist) *arises* out of the *midst* (the world of lawlessness)." This negates the claim that the restrainer represents the Holy Spirit being taken out of the way, for there is no *taken* nor *way* in this verse at all. Neither is removal indicated. It is not the rapture, but the rise of Antichrist that is taught here.

The second interpretation concedes that the Holy Spirit may be the restrainer, and that "becomes out of the midst" does indeed refer to the removal of the Spirit's restraint on Antichrist. But verse 7 does not teach that the Spirit is completely removed, nor that He reverts to a kind of Old Testament presence, nor that the Church is in any way connected with the action of this verse. Nowhere in Scripture is the Church the restrainer of Antichrist, and nowhere is the Spirit absent during the tribulation.

Just as race drivers are hindered until the flagman thrusts his green bandanna downward, so Antichrist must await the permission of a sovereign God to begin his ascent. The flagman does not leave the stadium at the start of the race, he just steps off the track. The Holy Spirit will be fully present in the Church during the tribulation, fully empowering the message of the Gospel, fully comforting the believers of that period. But whoever or whatever the restrainer is, the most important teaching of this chapter is that the rapture occurs at the *parousia* (v. 1, and I Thessalonians 4:15), and that the *parousia* occurs after Antichrist (v. 8). Here is the clearest statement on the time of the rapture in the whole of Scripture.

Although the identity of the restrainer may never be finally resolved, the time of the rapture is clearly foretold. And so, with undeniable clarity and candor, Paul in the Thessalonian

Epistles encourages us to be alert for the rise of Antichrist and the posttribulational coming of the Lord.

Footnotes

[10]Two eminent scholars who represent the pretribulation camp have suggested that the "falling away" should better be translated as "departure," specifically, the departure of the Church from the earth, thus proving their own position. It's an argument which defines the apostasy as the rapture, and leads to a rather gross confusion of Biblical themes. Examine it for yourself in *The Rapture Question,* by John Walvoord, p. 71-72.

[11]The first view is held by George E. Ladd in *The Blessed Hope,* p. 95; the second by Robert Gundry in *The Church and the Tribulation,* pp. 122-128.

Scripture reading

I Thessalonians 1:1-10, 2:19, 3:13, 4:13-18, 5:1-10; II Thessalonians 1:4-12; II Thessalonians 2:1-12.

Integration

1. Compare how the Lord's return is described in I Thessalonians 4:16-17 and in Matthew 24:30-31. Make a list of the events described in these two passages, and compare them for differences and similarities. Early-removal buffs claim that the former describes the pretribulation rapture, while the latter is the glorious return after the tribulation. Posttribbers say that Scripture speaks of one return, and that Paul describes in Thessalonians the same event that Jesus speaks of in the Gospel of Matthew. What do you find?

2. The idea of Christ coming as a "thief in the night" has been a common stumbling block to a clear posttribulational understanding of Jesus' return. Compare I Thessalonians 5:2-5 with Matthew 24:43, Luke 21:28, and Revelation 3:3. Who is surprised? Who is overtaken? Who is caught unaware?

3. The Bible teaches that at a certain point in time, Christians will be "gathered together" by the Lord. From II Thessalonians 2:1, Matthew 24:31, and Mark 13:27, is there any evidence to suggest that some believers are gathered seven years before other believers, or does Scripture speak of one gathering-together of all?

4. Compare the use of *parousia* (coming) in I Thessalonians 4:15, II Thessalonians 2:1, and 2:8. Does the rapture (ingathering) occur at the *parousia?* Does the *parousia* occur before or after Antichrist?

5. Our survey of New Testament teaching on the rapture is nearly half over. Make a list of questions that have come to mind so far, of difficulties that you see in the pre- or the posttrib point of view, and locate the answers either by review or by close study of remaining rapture texts.

Chapter Five

WIDE ANGLE:
THE TEACHINGS OF PAUL

In His Other Epistles

Paul was the apostle to the Gentiles, and in every sense a missionary-pastor to the New Testament Church. Surely, if the pretribulation rapture is a "Church truth" at all, it must be taught by Paul. Our examination of key rapture passages in the Thessalonian letters revealed that posttribulationism is certainly an intelligent option, and quite possibly the very point Paul was trying to make. But fairness prohibits us from arriving at a firm conclusion before all the evidence is in. Perhaps Paul has more to teach us in the remaining epistles, and we may yet find pretribulationism there. It is barely conceivable that Jesus should overlook such an important end-time truth, but hardly possible that Paul, the Church apostle, would fail to clearly teach the "rapture doctrine." Now we turn to Romans, I and II Corinthians, Ephesians, Philippians, Colossians, and the letters to Timothy and Titus. Open your Bible and discover what the Holy Spirit has revealed through this great pioneer of the faith concerning the return of the Lord Jesus Christ.

Romans 8:18-35—All creation groans

No other chapter in the Bible proclaims with such force and precision the great truths of redemption in Christ. It is a victorious chapter, finishing the "theological" part (chapters 1-

53

8) of the Roman letter. The Holy Spirit is constantly brought before our mind's eye. Previously mentioned only once in the book, here He is spoken of nineteen times. Freedom from condemnation, and liberty in the life-flow of the Spirit are resounding themes of Christian life, all wrapped in the context of God's sovereign design for us and the limitless love of our Lord Jesus Christ. The chapter divides into three units, each an aspect of the spiritual life, and the third a grand culmination of the Trinity's movement among the people of God:

Believer's Strength: The Indwelling Spirit, vs. 1-17.

Believer's Solace: Promised Glory, vs. 18-25.

Believer's Security: The Spirit's Intercessory Prayer, vs. 26-27; The Father's Providential Control, vs. 28-34; Christ's Inseparable Love, vs. 35-39.

The second part of our chapter outline gives another clue to the time of the rapture. Paul describes all created things as looking forward to deliverance from the bondage of corruption, groaning in pain until that time when redemption will be complete. The Christian described here is in greater agony than any other created thing, for he has experienced a foretaste of the heavenly fellowship. He has been given the Holy Spirit as a guarantee of adoption into God's family, and as a first fruit of the eternal experience. For any baseball fan who arrives at the park early enough to watch the pregame warm-up, nothing can satisfy the craving for action except the actual game itself.

Paul directs the attention of believers to that day when our bodies will be redeemed, and connects that fulfillment with the redemption of all creation. Although Paul's purpose is not to give specific time sequences, he clearly focuses attention on one event—the completion and goal of our hope. When Christ returns at the end of the tribulation, He will rapture and redeem His people, scourge the earth for its wickedness, and scour creation of its evil. What a great day that will be! We ought with patience to wait for it (v. 25).[12]

Paul also reminds us, in verse 20, of the tension inherent in following Christ's footsteps. Both man and creation share the common plight of unavoidable corruptibility. Bodies tire of age, brick and mortar eventually crumble, spirits grow heavy with the pain of lost loves, and dandelions creep into the sod. Yet there is hope that lifts the soul and looks to the day of redemption, not in the attitude of other-worldly escapism, but with the fortitude to persevere "unto the coming of the Savior." This tension between suffering and hope provides one key to our understanding of the Church in the tribulation. Christians are called to serve a Lord who suffered Himself. What servant can expect less than His master?

Verse's 35-39 assure us that no tribulation, however difficult, can separate us from Jesus' love. That promise has been good throughout history. It will be no less encouraging when persecution intensifies under Antichrist.

I Corinthians 1:7-8—Waiting for the revelation

By this time in our study, it should be clear that certain words and phrases are closely associated with pretribulation-ism, and others find frequent use among posttrib people. The "rapture," for example, is the first part of Christ's two-stage return (according to pretribbers), and the revelation is the second and final phase. Similarly, the "day of Christ" is said by traditional pretribbers to refer to the rapture, and the "day of the Lord" to the revelation. The pretrib phrases are not hard to keep straight if you remember that Jesus will come as Lord when He appears publicly at the end of the tribulation to judge Antichrist and establish His visible sovereignty; but He supposedly returns only as "Christ," i.e. Savior, to those who watch for Him in a secret and imminent coming before the tribulation. Paul's introduction to the Corinthian epistle spells trouble for both of these linguistic distinctions.

In verse 8, the apostle speaks of the culmination of history and the goal of Christian foresight as "the day of our Lord Jesus Christ." All three names of the Savior are used: Lord, Jesus and Christ. Distinctions between the day of Christ and the Day of the Lord disappear in Paul's combination of terms here. We suggest that they not only disappear, but never really were. The day of Christ is the day of the Lord—the great day when Jesus returns to meet His people and establish the righteousness of God.

In verse 7, the verbal distinction between the rapture and the revelation evaporates as Paul urges the Corinthian believers to wait for the "coming of our Lord." The word for "coming" here is *apokalupsis,* elsewhere translated "revelation." Paul is referring to none other than the posttribulational return of Christ—and he instructs the Christian Church to *wait for it!*

Many churches today, far from heeding Paul's message to eagerly await the *apokalupsis,* are looking forward to a return of Christ that neither Jesus nor Paul said anything about. The Corinthians were told to wait for Christ's revelation, and we find no reason to alter that instruction for the Church of the twentieth century.

I Corinthians 11:26—Remember till He comes

In Paul's well-known order of the Lord's Supper, he points again to the coming of the Lord Jesus, and talks as though the New Testament sacrament of communion should be practiced until that day arrives. The life of the Church will continue until the revelation of the Lord, although the tribulation will cause changes in form and style. Padded pews will be mere nostalgia for Christians of that age, but perhaps the vitality of Christian community will be recharged in their absence. The Lord's Supper shared during the tribulation will be a "time of remembering" unprecedented in history, for then His return will not be far off.

I Corinthians 15—In the twinkling of an eye

The church at Corinth had problems. Divisions within the fellowship, unchecked immorality, asceticism, gluttony at the Lord's table, and confusion over spiritual gifts were foremost concerns to the missionary Paul as he wrote to the fledgling assembly. But perhaps the most severe problem of all, due to its potential effects, was the questioning of the resurrection. So vital, in fact, was belief in Christ's resurrection to the spiritual health of the church that Paul could dismiss the entire

Christian enterprise as vanity, empty puffery, if indeed the Lord still lay in the grave.

Jesus' resurrection, the apostle teaches, is not only a cardinal doctrine, but a historical fact that gives substance to the Christian hope of immortality. If Christ be raised, then there is hope—beyond wishful thinking—for the resurrection of saints.

Verses 20-26 point to our redemption in Christ and resurrection at His coming. Christ Himself is the first fruit of resurrection. As the Author and Finisher of our faith, He leads the way for the resurrection of believers. Only one resurrection and translation of the righteous is foretold by Christ and Paul. All of the righteous will be included in this magnificent event—all the dead in Christ and all the living tribulation saints.

Verses 51-58 are an explicit statement on the rapture, and it is introduced as a mystery—a word that often refers to a truth that has not previously been fully revealed. Can we expect, then, that new information on the rapture is forthcoming?

"In a moment" (v. 52) is neither the brush-off of a TV football freak whose wife has just called him to dinner, nor is it Paul's way of saying the rapture could happen "at any moment," as early-removalists assert. The difference between "in a moment" and "at any moment" can be illustrated by the marriage ceremony. When the quivering groom and his resplendent queen say "I do," they become husband and wife. It would be proper to say that "in a moment" they become married. But to say that "at any moment" they could become married would be highly improper and slightly illegal. Certain formalities and registrations must occur before lovers can be wed.

Our illustration cannot be pushed too far, but it does serve to say that "in a moment" refers to a specific time, not to the possibility of something happening "at any moment." Likewise, "in the twinkling of an eye" draws attention to the quickness of the event, but not to its nearness or imminence. Christ has said that certain things must come to pass before He returns. But far from being able to predict the exact time of His

57

coming (for no man knows the hour), we shall be obedient to the Lord's wishes if we wait, watch and work until He returns with the speed of an eyelid's flutter.

"At the last trump" reminds us of the same phrase in Matthew 24 and I Thessalonians 4, where we discovered it as an element of Christ's posttribulational return. (And *last* most certainly means last.) Together with Revelation 11, we get the picture of that final trumpet blast announcing the approach of Christ. The dead in Christ will be resurrected and the living in Christ will be translated at the last trump—a clear indication that the rapture and the revelation are simultaneous events that mark the closing moments of the world we know.

Verse 52 teaches that at the moment of resurrection, the dead will be raised and given eternal bodies of glory (Philippians 3:21), and the living will be instantly translated from their mortal frames to the same glorious bodies without experiencing death. What thrill, excitement, comfort and peace believers can enjoy as we anticipate the moment of the return of Christ in glory.

The specific time element of the resurrection is implied in verse 54. "So when this corruptible (the dead) shall have put on incorruption (resurrection), and this mortal (the living) shall have put on immortality (translation), then shall be brought to pass the saying that is written (in Isaiah 25:8): 'Death is swallowed up in victory.' (And in Hosea 13:14) 'O death, where is thy sting? O grave, where is thy victory?' " Here Paul links the New Testament teaching on resurrection with the Old Testament promises of victory—which always are stationed at the glorious coming of Messiah, after Israel's tribulation, at the beginning of the kingdom of peace. Paul locates the hope of both Testaments "at the last trump" and salutes it as the victory of Jesus Christ. What grand unity in God's economy of redemption. Perhaps this unity is the "mystery" that Paul was commissioned to deliver.

Verse 58 is a profound call to righteous living in view of the certainty of our victory in Christ. Too often our minds dwell on the speculative and predictive aspects of end-times truth and we become absorbed in futuristic daydreaming. Let Paul's admonition to the Corinthians accompany every end-times Bible study and discussion session. Christians do not live in the future. We can do no more than maximize each day's potentials, adopting an attitude of steadfast resilience to every lesser goal than the abounding work of the Redeemer, "forasmuch as you know that your labor is not in vain in the Lord."

II Corinthians 5:10-11—The judgment seat of Christ

No time or place element is mentioned in this reference to the judgment seat of Christ, so pre- and posttribbers alike can locate it according to their peculiar schemes. We should note, however, the "terror of the Lord" in verse 11, and recall that judgment and the Lord's sword of righteousness will fall at His posttribulation return. No doubt the "terror" has a broader meaning than simply Christ's apocalyptic housecleaning, but our secondary application fits in well with other passages which more pointedly describe the time of the rapture.

Ephesians 1:13-14, 4:30—Sealed to redemption

These few verses speak of the Holy Spirit's seal upon the Christian until the "day of redemption" and the "redemption of the purchased possession." The words parallel Christ's teaching in Luke 21:28: "When these things begin to come to pass, then look up . . . for your *Redeemer* draweth nigh," and Paul's pen in Romans 8:22-23: "The whole creation . . . and we ourselves . . . waiting for the adoption, to wit, the *redemption* of our body." Clearly our hope looks to the day of redemption, which by all other Scriptures is the day of resurrection at the return of Christ following the tribulation. The Christian is constantly urged to fix his hope on that one great return.

Philippians 1:6, 2:16, 3:20-21—God's good works

The story of religion can be told almost entirely in terms of man's attempt to satisfy the gods, and thereby to insure his own satisfaction. One of the traditional ways of winning the gods' favors is by being a good boy as much of the time as possible. Christian groups sometimes have seized upon this well-

59

intentioned but misguided human urge and have built a road to heaven out of good works. Nothing could be further from the Bible's story of redemption—the gift of God, not a matter of earning forgiveness by clean living, but of grace, God's undeserved favor, and repentance for the shortcomings inherent and too plentiful in all of us.

Paul, in his letter to Philippi, makes it clear that God is doing a good work in us (rather than vice versa), and He will continue to do it until the day of Jesus Christ (1:6). Four verses later he repeats the same phrase: " . . . that you may approve the things that are excellent, in order to be sincere and blameless until the day of Christ." In 2:16, Paul anticipates his joy "in the day of Christ" for the faithful discipleship of Philippian believers. But nowhere does Paul teach that the day of Christ is different from the day of the Lord.

In fact, Philippians 3:20-21 establishes our citizenship in heaven, "from which also we eagerly wait for a Savior, the Lord Jesus Christ," who will not only transform our bodies into the likeness of His own, but will "subject all things to Himself." The truth woven into Romans 8 appears again—Jesus will both resurrect His people at His coming, and redeem creation. And all this is related in Philippians to the day of Christ.

The day of Christ, then, cannot be a subtle designation for a secret, phase-one rapture, but in every instance should be taken to coincide with the great return of Jesus Christ as Redeemer and Lord of *all the earth.*

Colossians 3:1-4—The upward look
Christian discipleship demands a radical reorientation in lifestyle and priorities. In terms of ego-advancement and self-preservation, we are like dead men. But in terms of availability to serve as the "salt and light" of the world, channeling Christ's message into our respective spheres of influence, we are alive unto God. Paul identifies life with Christ Himself, and reminds Christians again that Christ's glory will be shared by God's people when He is revealed.

Early-removal brethren find here a reference to the

60

appearance of the saints in heaven at the time of the rapture. Surely, Christ is in heaven (where He must remain until the times of restitution of all things prophesied), and Christ is certainly and in every way the foundation of our life (John 14:6). To these truths Colossians 3:4 adds that when Christ shall appear, we also shall appear with Him glorified, that is, in our glorified bodies. The phrase "in glory" is more than an adjective describing *where* we will appear. "Glory," as used here, is not a reference to heaven, but to the glorification of Jesus Christ when "He comes in flaming fire, with all His mighty angels . . . to be glorified in his saints" (II Thessalonians 2:7-10). The passage will not bear the weight of pretribulationism.

I Timothy 6:13-15—Keep the commandment

"Don't keep the faith, give it away" is a wise half-truth, for unless we hold the faith in its pure and unmuddled truth, we will have nothing of substance to give away at all. Timothy's high charge to keep the commandment, to fight the good fight of faith and lay hold of the eternal life to which He was called (v. 12), was put in effect "until the appearing of our Lord Jesus Christ, which He will bring about at the proper time—He who is the blessed and only Sovereign, the King of kings and Lord of lords."

Simply but clearly, Paul is instructing his young disciple to keep the commandments of God, not until some secret rapture of the Church, but until the appearing, the visible manifestation (*epiphaneia*), of our Lord Jesus Christ, which by all definitions is at the consummation of the age.

Verse 15 provides a close parallel to a passage we shall examine shortly, Revelation 19:11-16. There we find a vivid word-picture of the Lord's return with His heavenly armies to judge and make war, to rule with a rod of iron, to pour out His wrath; and His name is *King of kings, and Lord of lords*. Both passages carry the identical, majestic title.

Paul would hardly have misled Timothy by encouraging him to fix his spiritual sight on Christ's return in glory if, in fact, there was to be a secret return prior to the public one. No, the Apostle points Timothy's attention to the visible, posttribulational manifestation of our Lord, and commands him and us to keep the commandment of God *until* that appearing.

II Timothy 4:1—The judge is coming
Paul speaks here of the judgment seat of Christ, before which we must all appear (II Corinthians 5:10), thus tying the judgment of the saints with Christ's appearing and kingdom—a most definite posttribulational statement. How different is this view from that which would place the judgment seat of Christ in heaven immediately after the pretribulation rapture and during the tribulation. The Bible states clearly that the saints are judged at the appearing of Christ and His kingdom.

The same truth is echoed in verses 7-8, where Paul foresees the granting of rewards "at that day"—the day when those who "love His appearing" will likewise be blessed, the day unto which Jesus is able to keep all we have committed to Him (II Timothy 1:12). Modern attempts to bisect the appearing of Christ and speed the day of reward to a pretribulational "secret appearing" must reckon with Paul's rather precise positioning of that day at the visible revelation of Christ.

Titus 2:11-15—Our blessed hope
The world's greatest love stories are tales of hope. The Bible far surpasses earthly literature both in its elevation of love and in its certainty of hope. "For God so loved the world" . . . "nothing shall separate us from the love of Christ" . . . "God is love" are themes that raise the song of love between a sovereign Creator and His fallen people to a crescendo greater than all other songs. Love's hope, for the Christian, is not a fancy or whim, not a dream. It is an anchor to the spirit. But it is still hope. We do not tote our faith in God's promise of eternal life as though we had already died and could verify from personal experience that heaven is really there. We hope.

In Titus 2:13, Paul centers the Christian's hope in the "glorious appearing of the great God and our Savior Jesus

Christ." Verses just before (11,12) remind us that hope is not just forward-looking, but takes practical hold of each daily moment in obedient, disciple-like living.

It is entirely proper that we should "look" for that "blessed hope," and on that all Christians agree. It is, however, on the definition of that hope that we differ. To some, the "blessed hope" is Paul's subtle way of pointing our gaze to the first phase (pretribulation rapture) of a two-stage return. The comma which divides verse 13 in the King James version has become inspired proof that the second phase, the "glorious appearing," is properly distinguished from the first.

How does Paul define the "hope"? The verse is properly translated without the comma and without the second article "the." It reads: "Looking for the blessed hope and appearing of the glory of our great God and Savior Jesus Christ."[13] Paul identifies the blessed hope with the glorious appearing as the one event worth looking for. The connective *and*, which joins two nouns, means "even" or "which is," as in Matthew 24:3 and II Thessalonians 2:1. There is no grammatical distinction here and, up to this point, there has been found no Biblical distinction. Rapture and revelation are the same event.

The word *epiphaneia*, which means "visible manifestation" and is here translated as "appearing," forms another link in the chain of Bible texts that insist we identify the blessed hope with the posttribulational return of Christ. In I and II Timothy, the "appearing" is connected with Jesus' kingdom and rewards, and in II Thessalonians 2:8 it is linked with the destruction of Antichrist. It is not enough to say that at the pretribulation rapture, Christ "appears" in His glory to the Church, for He taught that "all the tribes of the earth . . . shall see the Son of man coming in the clouds of heaven with power and great glory." It is the posttrib coming that will be visible, and only it can be properly called the "appearing," the *epiphaneia*. It is indeed our blessed hope.

Footnotes

[12]Amillenialists will lay eager claim to the promise of worldwide renewal at the return of Christ. Premillenialists, too, can anticipate a great cleansing and a fresh

beginning after the Lion of Judah wields His sharp sword at the culmination of the tribulation.

[13]George E. Ladd, *The Blessed Hope*, p. 157, and John Walvoord, *The Rapture Question*, p. 81. Both Ladd (posttrib) and Walvoord (pretrib) agree at this point.

Scripture reading

Romans 8:18-35; 1 Corinthians 1:7-8, 11:26, 15; II Corinthians 5:10-11; Ephesians 1:13-14, 4:30; Philippians 1:6, 2:16, 3:20-21; Colossians 3:1-4; 1 Timothy 6:13-15; II Timothy 4:1; Titus 2:11-15.

Integration

1. Compare all you have learned about Jesus' teachings on the rapture with all you now know about Paul's approach to the issue.

2. What are some of the guidelines for living mentioned in connection with the return of Christ (for example, review I Corinthians 15:58 and Titus 2:11-13).

3. Remembering all the details as you study the Bible often can be difficult, particularly when we jump from one passage to another such as we did in this chapter. You will find it helpful to do an analysis of the verses under study, following the example given below. If you are in a discussion group, each member could take one of the passages under study, then share the results with all.

Titus 2:13:

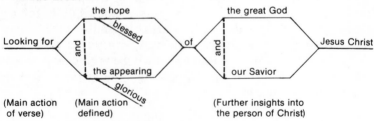

4. List and compare the insights gleaned from your analysis above. Spend a season in prayer over them. Ask God to build you up in truth—then put the truth into action.

Chapter Six

EXTENDED WIDE ANGLE: OTHER NEW TESTAMENT WRITINGS

In Acts, Hebrews, Peter, John and Jude

Christians never cease to wonder at the unity and integrity of Holy Scripture. That one theme should predominate, coherently and consistently, in a book written by so many hands over a span of so many years is an awesome matter. God Himself gave the Book to us. Jesus verified its truth by His own extensive use of it. And even though we hold its truth in dearest esteem, we would have due cause to question should we find contradictions and unresolved disputes among its several authors. If, in fact, Jesus taught one return and Paul taught two, or if John's blessed hope was at variance with Peter's, we would be in trouble. Agnostics and humanists would stand a good chance of reducing Christianity to a man-conceived religion, and churchmen would no longer have authoritative recourse in a divinely-inspired Word.

We turn now to other New Testament writers, always in the confidence that their teachings will corroborate the precious doctrines learned before, adding insight or perhaps definition, and persistently reinforcing the call to discipleship sounded first by the Lord Himself.

Acts 1:3-12—In like manner will He return
The book of Acts has little to say about the coming of the Lord, inasmuch as Luke's primary purpose centered on the early history of the Church. But in a few select passages, we

find some important evidence in our search for the time of the rapture.

Acts 1 records the final conversation between Christ and His disciples, and a familiar question comes up once again: "Lord, is it at this time you are restoring the kingdom to Israel?"

Jesus' reply was twofold. First, it is the Father's business to set dates and times, not the business of men, either to do it or to know it. Second, the disciples were given work to do—the extensive job of taking the message of redemption to Jerusalem, Judea, Samaria, and throughout the earth. Christ was simply echoing His words on Olivet: "This gospel of the kingdom shall be preached in all the world for a witness unto all nations; and then shall the end come." Apparently Jesus had in mind a certain length of time needed to accomplish the task. It is enough to say that Jesus did not give the impression, either during His ministry or at His ascension, that His return would come *at any moment.*

As Jesus rises beyond the sight of the gathered disciples, two heavenly beings speak words that send the group back to Jerusalem with great joy: "This same Jesus . . . shall so come in like manner as ye have seen Him go into heaven." If their words were more than science fiction, and we believe they were, Jesus' return will be visible, from heaven, with clouds, to the earth, and in glory (I Timothy 3:16). This is consistent with all that Jesus taught, and with the Old Testament prophecies concerning His return in power and glory at the end of the age. Note especially that the center of attention here is on His return, and not the rapture of the saints, because the rapture will occur *as part of* that return. Note also that Christ speaks of His return in conjunction with the fulfillment of The Great Commission.

A plank heard often from early-removal campaigners is that Christ will come into the air for the Church, and then return to heaven for the duration of the tribulation. But if Jesus is really to return as He ascended, then He must return all the way to the Mount of Olives (compare v. 12 with Zechariah 14:4). No Scripture up to this point teaches that the air is the terminus of His coming.

Acts 2:17-20—Peter speaks

Sanguine Peter's first sermon, begun without the aid of an opening hymn or offertory solo, quotes from the prophet Joel concerning the outpouring of the Holy Spirit in the last days with attendant prophecies, visions and dreams. Verse 19 mentions those specific signs which will immediately precede the return of Christ as spoken of in Matthew 24—signs in heaven and earth, the darkening of the sun, moon and stars. Of special importance is the phrase in verse 20: "before that great and notable day of the Lord come." These heavenly signs must precede the day of the Lord.

Some scholars have developed a working definition of the "day of the Lord" that we have mentioned earlier. It bears repeating since, if correct, it allows for a secret, pretribulation return despite the obvious clamor that will precede the coming Lord according to the present passage. The day of the Lord, it is claimed, begins with the rapture, includes the time of tribulation, and culminates with the return of Christ in glory.

To this we make a stubborn reply, "Show me!" The day of the Lord is not an extensive, long-term process, but is clearly after the aforementioned signs and cosmic wonders quite noisy, quite visible, and quite open to the public.

Acts 3:18-21—A time for restitution

Repentance too often is a hasty afterthought in contemporary gospelizing. Much more attractive is the appeal to native self-interest, and the offer of eternal bliss together with abundant living now. These sometimes shade the reality of human sin.

Repentance was the first word for Peter in his Pentecost sermon and again here—a precedent that must not fall. Almost in the same breath the swarthy fisherman adds, "And he shall send Jesus Christ . . . whom the heaven must receive until the times of restitution of all things." The hope of Jesus' return was not far from the early appeal for repentance and conversion.

Important to our study is the truth that Christ is now in heaven, and must remain there until the world is restored and His reign begins. Recall that Romans 8 pictures all of creation groaning for the revealing of the sons of God. Surely Jesus will not institute His reign before the tribulation. Then how can He leave heaven to rapture the Church? The early-removal theory says He must, but Acts 3:21 suggests that Jesus is to remain in heaven until His glorious return ends the age and begins the one to come.

Hebrews 9:28—The second appearing

Here is the only passage in Scripture which uses the word *"second"* in relation to Christ's return. The term "second coming," although a helpful tool for us, does not appear in God's Word.

This verse does not bear on our attempt to locate the time of the rapture, but it is useful to note that the specific term "second" is employed to describe the Lord's return. The German philosopher, Ludwig Wittgenstein, once said, in effect, that language is really what you make it. He meant that words derive their meaning from the particular "language game" in which they are used, and that as long as everyone plays by the same rules, no one should get angry.[14]

So we find one game going on which says that "second" really means "second-third," or "second, one—second, two," or "second first, second second."

Wait a second! Second means second! When Christ's second coming is spoken of in terms of His appearing unto salvation, there should be only one language game on the field. Jesus' "appearing" is always posttribulational, and the second time He appears will therefore be posttribulational, too. No third or fourth comings allowed.

Hebrews 10:12-13—Enemies for footstools

Again Scripture locates Christ in heaven, here more specifically at the right hand of God, until the day when He triumphs over the forces of evil in every place. To say that Jesus can leave His throne for a quick trip to midatmosphere, then return to His designated place by the Father, is to insert a voyage that Scripture disallows. And who is the Author of Scripture if not God Himself?

Jesus said that He would return at the consummation of the age, and that His coming would be a time of triumph for righteousness and judgment for wrong. Perhaps this approaching climax is what causes Satan to tremble in belief (James 2:19). What enemy of Christ will stand when His sabre slashes the earth (Revelation 19:15)?

I Peter 1:7—Tried by fire

Far from a flighty fixation on bubbly living, Scripture writers consistently communicated the tense and often painful struggle out of which their faith was molded. Here Peter claims that faith tested by suffering is made of stronger stuff than gold tried by fire, and such faith will be found "unto praise and honor and glory at the *appearing* of Jesus Christ." This familiar term, *apokalupsis,* refers to the public unveiling of Christ at His return in power and glory after the tribulation. Peter teaches that the trial of our faith will continue until the revelation, when the true carats of faith will be fully measured.

I Peter 1:13—Grace at the revelation

Peter is instructing the Christian elect concerning their attitude until the time of the end—settled minds, serious thinking, full of hope. He also instructs that a specific grace will be brought to us at the revelation of Jesus—once again, a reference to the visible, public unveiling, and return in power and glory.

I Peter 4:12-13—Partners in Christ's sufferings

The union of the Christian with Christ is never so emotionally real as during times of suffering, and so it should not surprise us to hear the disciple who was so intent on following the Savior claim that suffering was a reason for exceeding joy. Peter knew personally the "fiery trials" of early Christianity, and he speaks empathetically to large concentrations of Christians in our day who sustain similar oppression.

Peter's call to all generations of the Church is one of joy in adversity. How different is the modern notion that unless we are looking for an escape from tribulation, we are not in the proper (and spiritual) frame of mind. Paul made the connection between suffering and victory even more direct when he said, in II Timothy 2:12: "If we suffer, we shall also reign with Him."

Notice that the word *apokalupsis* (revelation) occurs again as the time when our joy will be full. At the public unveiling of Christ—His glorious return—the Christian's joy is made complete. No matter how fiery the trial, and Peter knew well how hot it could get, the follower of Jesus takes confidence that the One who owns him will one day revisit a spiritually desolate planet to give tangible proof to the promises of Scripture. That Peter draws attention to the "fiery trial" preceding that day should be enough to nullify popular hopes of an early exit. Although the final tribulation may not be the specific time period in view here, it certainly qualifies under Peter's description. When the charge is made: "How could looking for the coming of the Lord *after* the tribulation in any sense be the blessed hope, a comforting hope, and a joyful hope?" we have but to turn to I Peter 4:13 for the ready answer.

I Peter 5:4—When the Chief Shepherd appears
Jesus is called by many names in the Bible. We find Him spoken of as the Son of man, the Door, the Bread, the Vine, the Author, the Captain and, most poignantly, the Shepherd. He is the Shepherd who guards the flock, whose voice is known by the sheep, who leads into green pastures. If the Bible were being written today, perhaps the name Good Shepherd would be replaced by Good Coach—a leader of the team in the scrimmage of life. Peter connects the appearance of the Good Shepherd with the distribution of untarnishable crowns to the righteous elect.

Peter's teaching fits well with the words of the Lord in Matthew 16:28: "For the Son of man shall come in the glory of His Father, with His angels, and *then* He shall reward every man according to his works," and in Luke 14:14: "For thou shalt be recompensed at the resurrection of the just." Rewards are given not at an unprescribed midair meeting before the tribulation, but at the public appearing, the glorious unveiling, of the Lord.

Peter wrote to fortify the spiritual muscle of scattered Christians. Instead of mentioning the possibility of a quick release through a sudden return of Christ, he firmly prepares them for increased suffering ahead. Yet all the while, rejoicing, gladness, and hope are a prayer's breath away. Grace, crowns, glory, praise and honor will accompany the revelation of Jesus Christ from heaven—the *second* time.

II Peter 3:10-13—The day of the Lord

Again the phrase "a thief in the night" describes the Lord's coming. Consistent with all the other occurrences of this metaphor, we find that He will come as a thief to the "scoffers in the last days" (v. 3), to the "willingly ignorant" (v. 5), and to "some men" (v. 9). Children of God, however, walk in the day and in the light (I Thessalonians 2:4-5).

How often have we heard that the "thief" comes at the rapture? Yet it is not the rapture, but the "day of the Lord" (defined by most pretribulationists as the posttrib return in glory) that Peter mentions here—not the "day of Christ" at all (which again, by pretrib definition, is the rapture). And the day of the Lord, it must be remembered, will be heralded by quite visible signs (Acts 2:20), which will signal the return of Christ to all who watch for them. Christians will not be overtaken by stealth and caprice as a thief pounces on his loot. Peter is talking about the posttribulational day of the Lord.

Because the Lord is coming, we ought to walk in holiness and do our business with uncolored integrity. The moral aspect of the Lord's return never fails to find a place in end-times Bible passages. We are never to look up and stand still waiting, but always to watch and walk, smartly working.

Before the atom's power was known, verse 7 must have seemed possible only through a direct fiat of God. But none can now intelligently question man's own capacity to destroy himself should the wrong people make the wrong decisions at the wrong time. Our penchant for getting involved in wars, and

71

too seldom resolving the reasons for them, should leave no one with doubts about the possibility that these fearsome predictions will be literally fulfilled.

In verse 12, we discover the disarming truth that Christians should be hastening the day of God, as though mere men could influence the universe's timetable. Christ commanded us to preach the Gospel to every nation, land, tribe and tongue. Until this is done, He cannot return. The job will be accomplished, we know, because in Revelation we read that people from "all nations, all kindreds, all people, and all tongues" are among the redeemed (Revelation 7:9). Christ said that "first the gospel of the kingdom must be preached to all nations, and then the end shall come" (Matthew 24:14). So Peter's lesson here relates to our obedience in fulfilling The Great Commission. By preaching the Gospel in worldwide evangelism, we actually are hastening the day when the Lord can come. It is not enough to "prepare the Church for the rapture." Our job description reads: "Go ye therefore and teach all nations . . . and lo, I am with you always, even unto the end of the age."

Verse 13 is another pungent reminder that Christians are to live holy lives, not because of a threat that the Lord may come at any moment, but in light of God's righteous judgment on the wicked, and the eternal rewards in that "day of God" when we shall forever be joined with Him in the new heavens and the new earth.

I John 3:2-3—We shall see Him

As a father writes to a distant son, so John speaks the words of God to us in these three brief letters. If any New Testament writer comes close to using poetry as the genré of divine truth, it is John. In the tones of a gentle pastor, John makes us feel whole and human while calling us little children. We don't seem to mind.

John's end-times message for us is intimate and hope-filled. We are to become like Christ at the Lord's appearing. Christ presently is hidden from the world, as we are (v. 1), but when He appears and is revealed, we also shall be revealed (Romans 8:19): "The creation waits for the manifestation, or revealing,

72

of the sons of God." "We shall be like Him" rehearses the glorification and translation of the saints mentioned in I Corinthians 15:51-52.

Notice that the emphasis is not on our dying and going to heaven, nor on an imminent rapture of the Church, but always on the appearing of Christ. This appearing is again made the action-center, the vortex, the prime incentive for right holy living, and we might without hesitation say that that includes evangelism as well as pietism.

Paul taught that our vision is presently clouded, as though we were attempting to see through a darkened mirror. But then, at the day when partial endowment is cast aside for the fullness of God's light, we shall see Him face to face (I Corinthians 13:12). Who would keep an appointment like that in soiled dungarees? "Every man that hath this hope in him purifieth himself, even as He is pure."

Jude 14-15—A warning to the ungodly

It was characteristic of Bible evangelists to spare few words in warning sinners that the price of indifference and frivolity was high. From the first human generations, the warning is clearly sounded, and Enoch's biting words have kept pace with changing societies ever since. We would not want to "turn the reader off" by a monologue of threats and admonitions, but to remind all who have not sought the Lord that procrastination in eternal matters is a risky trait with irrevocable consequences. Christ will return, and the offer of pardon will then become the pronouncement of judgment.

Have you spoken a "harsh thing" against God? Have you done an "ungodly" deed? Only great fools need convincing that if a holy God exists at all, we cannot tote our pomp before Him. Be among the saints at His coming by surrendering your future, and confessing your past, to the Lord Jesus Christ.

Footnotes

[14]We admit to a rather crude paraphrase of Wittgenstein's line of thought. We do not minimize the German thinker's contribution to linguistic analysis.

Scripture reading

Acts 1:3-12, 2:17-20, 3:18-21; Hebrews 9:28, 10:12-13; I Peter 1:7, 1:13, 4:12-13, 5:4; II Peter 3:10-13; I John 3:2-3; Jude 14-15.

Integration

1. We have noted that suffering is a recurring theme among New Testament writings. Discuss and determine your personal attitude toward suffering. Suffering should hold neither morbid attractiveness, nor be a cause of timid fear. We ought to be able to handle it with more "exceeding joy" than stoics meeting their fate. But be careful. A misplaced "joy in suffering" becomes ego-infatuating.

2. It often is possible to read Scripture but grossly misunderstand its meaning if the context is not considered. (You've heard that the Bible can be used to prove almost anything?) If you are in a group, divide this chapter's Bible portions among the members, and "digest" the surrounding verses. Summarize and report. Determine if your understanding of the context casts new slants on your interpretation of particular verses.

3. If possible, read a chapter or two of early church history and discover how the first New Testament churchmen faced the tribulation of their day. Being a Christian did not really become fashionable until Constantine made it the official religion of the Roman Empire in the fourth century, so you have nearly 300 years of persecution history to draw from. If medieval or perhaps modern history is your bag, there are plenty of good titles and courageous personalities to learn from there.

4. Continue your list of moral values associated with the Lord's second coming. Passages studied in this chapter are full of instructions on how a Christian should live in view of the end times. (Make sure you *are* one before you try to live like one. The reverse is not only boring, but could lead to some dangerous miscalculations on your real standing before God.)

Chapter Seven

FOCUS: THE RETURN
IN REVELATION 19-20

"His name is called the Word of God"

Revelation is probably the most puzzling book in the entire Bible. Its symbols and images dance across the twenty-two chapters like odd-shaped jigsaw pieces. They challenge the most adroit student to arrange them in an understandable way.

Many Christians give up on Revelation, yet it is the only book which specifically promises blessing to the one who reads it (1:3). It also is the only Bible book that contains a specific warning against tampering with it. "Neither add nor subtract from this book," sounds the heavenly angel as John concludes his report in chapter 22. We apply that warning to all of Scripture and regard the entire Bible as God's unique and authoritative message to men. Yet it is significant that the warning should appear in Revelation. No other book has attracted such a variety of interpretations. Even today scholars put forth tentative solutions and likely answers to the many questions that John's visions raise.

No Bible student should be discouraged by symbolism, nor should a Christian intent on learning God's Word pass over Revelation because other Scriptures are less difficult. The book of Revelation contains great lessons in Christian conduct, Christian hope, the ideal Christian church, and the sovereign deity of the Lord Jesus Christ. To learn the meaning of Revelation is to gain insight into some of the deepest and most practical truths God has given us. To avoid the book is to stymie growth in Christian maturity. Let the picturesque symbols speak to you in the beauty of their poetry. Pursue their meaning with the same unquenchable tenacity that Zaccheus used to catch a glimpse of the Messiah when His natural line of vision was all but blocked.

Bible students should not be discouraged with tentative answers. Satisfaction often is limited to tentative conclusions, particularly in the secondary details and obscure word-pictures that regularly appear in Revelation. Tentative answers, in those cases, are not a sign of weakness, spiritual ambivalence, or mental dullness. Rather, we can confidently speak about symbolic meanings that appear to be consistent with other Scripture relevant to the symbol, and respectfully permit a certain latitude for differing alternatives among the community of believers.

The difficulty of interpreting symbols is the reason for so many divergent explanations of the book of Revelation.

Preterists insist that the book has meaning only for the churches in Asia Minor to which it was addressed. They discount prophetic value, and claim that the symbols, though clear to first-century believers, have lost their practical value for Christians of the twentieth century.

Historicists attempt to apply the symbols to historical characters and events surrounding major movements in the development of the Church. Scholars who so explain Revelation have found agreement between themselves to be a rare commodity, and the maze of potential historical applications often muddy the waters rather than clear them.

Idealists, or *allegorists,* wish to give broad spiritual applications to the startling visual images that appeared to John. Forces of good are represented by the triumphant Lamb who returns to execute judgment and sustain victory over the forces of evil, represented by the beast, harlot, and false prophet. While idealists avoid the petty battles of historicists, and retain the relevancy that preterists eschew, they must answer the charge of loosely handling Biblical words and phrases which refer to specific personages, events and time relationships.

Futurists have fought for the prophetic value of Revelation, maintaining that chapter four to the end is a glimpse into the climax of world history and the final state of the new heavens and new earth.

We hold, despite in-fighting among futurists regarding interpretational details, that this last method of studying Revelation is the most profitable. We recognize that the book must have been understood and appreciated by Christians of the first century (Revelation was probably written around A.D. 95). At the same time, its symbols certainly describe the victory of good over evil, specifically in the victory of Christ over Satan. And perhaps early Christians found consolation in identifying the symbols with historical figures, thereby strengthening their determination to remain loyal under persecution to the God who promised to lead all His people to victory and glory. But the main import, the chief lesson of Revelation, is that Jesus Christ will personally reign.

God's plan for history will be fulfilled in the glorious return of Christ. Satan and Antichrist will be judged without parole, along with all who have not the Spirit of God as their seal and pledge. Persecution will accelerate as the return approaches— and we soon shall see who it is that must endure it.

The great debate under study here, of course, is the time of the Church's rapture, whether it precedes or coincides with the return of Christ. We must again emphasize that this is the most practical, the most pressing question in any study of the end times. Surely the millennial debate in Revelation 20 has importance. But between the two most likely possibilities (amillennialism and premillennialism) there is little practical difference. When we are with Christ, whether in a temporary millennial kingdom or in the new heavens and new earth itself, we shall know joy in fellowship and worship. The setting is incidental; the Savior's presence is sufficient.

Chapters 19 and 20 focus on the glorious and awe-inspiring return of Christ, a theme too powerful for ordinary prose. Christ is described in John's vision as a conqueror on a white steed, sword flashing from his mouth, followed by a multitude of heavenly attendants. A careful reading and reverent study of

77

this prophetic narrative will compel us to bend the knee and confess that Jesus is indeed Lord. It should also lead us to further evidence on the time of His coming.

Chapter 19 begins with resounding hallelujahs for the victory of Christ over evil, then describes the marriage of the Lamb, reports the return of Christ and the ensuing battle, and leads into the millennial narrative and great white throne judgment of chapter 20.

Revelation 19:1-10—The marriage supper of the Lamb

As the scene unfolds and the sky opens for the descent of the conquering Lamb, the heavenly multitude, together with the twenty-four elders and four living beings (mentioned in the heavenly scene of chapters 4-5) join in praise and song for the sovereignty of the Lamb now manifest (v. 4-6). As though anticipating the aftermath of battle, these heavenly observers sing to a victory that is sure to come; then announce in the next refrain that a binding love is about to be consummated in the marriage of the Lamb.

Many distinctions are attempted between those invited to the supper (v. 9) and those who actually participate (v. 7). The Bride of Christ has been restricted, by early removal advocates, to believers of the Church age. After all, the argument goes, is it right to confuse the bride with invited guests? While Scripture abounds with valid and edifying distinctions between people of one type or another, even between themselves (see I Corinthians 12), in this case a distinction has been fabricated for expediency in promoting a point of view.

A host of problems are solved for early removalists if distinct groups can be identified at the marriage feast. There at the banquet table sits the Church, all who have been saved by faith and raptured prior to the tribulation. Next, standing on the outer periphery and serving as witnesses to the wedding are the saints of the Old Testament whose entry was gained by whatever salvatory means were operative during their particular lifetime. And moving in and out of the festival hall are the attendants, martyred saints of the tribulation who responded to the message of the kingdom preached by Jewish

78

missionaries during the final years of evil.

Where distinctions are supported by Scripture, let them stand. Here, the distinctions are dubious, and we suggest that the bride of the Lamb is the whole company of those who have been reconciled to God through Christ since the Creator first said, "Let there be . . ."

The holy Writer of Revelation has not given us the language of a book on systematic theology. Images pass before the mind's eye, each with a message intended to be understood, but not with the precision ˜of tightly reasoned logic. The language of Revelation permits different metaphors to describe the same person or group. The One who appears as a lion and a lamb (Revelation 5:5,6) is the same person to which all true prophecy must bear testimony (19:10). It is not inconceivable, then, that all God's children should be described as both the bride and the invited guests.

A perceptive reader may ask: How can the marriage supper happen before the rapture and in the height of tribulation, since many Bible students maintain a strict chronology in these chapters? But notice that the hallelujahs announcing the beginning of Christ's reign already have been shouted (v. 6), and Christ is now reigning. It is after His reign commences that the marriage supper is held. John places the events of verses 6-10 after the events of the following verses. Christ will return in triumph to reign as King and Lord, and then all the redeemed will sit down with Him for that festive feast to celebrate His return—that final victory over Antichrist himself.

Revelation 19:11-16—The heavens open

The seals, trumpets and bowls of Revelation are finished, and the nameless Sovereign who is called the Word of God breaks through the hemisphere in mighty terror for the nations, and happy reunion for His people. This is the revelation of Christ foretold in Revelation 1:1. This is Christ the Word, of John 1:1. With Him come armies from heaven (mentioned before in Revelation 15:6, Matthew 13:49; 24:31) to gather the elect from the four corners of earth and heaven. These are perhaps the angels of II Thessalonians 1:7 who accompany their Captain when He is "revealed from heaven with all His mighty angels," and again the angels of I Thessalonians 4:16 which sound the victory call. Perhaps these also include the spirits of saints who have died in Christ and will now assume resurrection bodies.

This is the coming of Christ to which all the hallelujahs in Revelation point. Verse 15—"from His mouth comes a sharp sword"—is a close parallel to II Thessalonians 2:8, which forecasts the doom of Antichrist: "then that lawless one will be revealed whom the Lord will slay with the breath of His mouth *and bring to an end by the appearance of His coming."* This return of Christ occurs after the futile brutality of the beast. Antichrist's destruction and the union of Christ with His Church inspire the hallelujah songs of history. The hope of God's people has been vindicated.

Revelation 20:1-6—A conflict avoided, a certainty revealed

Disputes over Bible teaching on the end times often have centered on the twentieth chapter of Revelation, since here premillennialists draw their ammunition for a 1000-year earthly reign, amillennialists traverse the historical timeline to suggest the 1000 years as a symbol of the Church age, and postmillennialists propose a similar symbol but with a happy ending—the Christianization of the world.

We intend to stick with our initial postulate and bypass the question. The return of Christ is the hope of the Church, and after His return—whether to inaugurate a long rule here or to usher in the new heaven and new earth—life with Him will be enough. Where Christ and His people are together, hope is fulfilled and joy is consummated. The geographical and political environment seem insignificant in comparison.

Nevertheless, our second postulate—that Christ's one and only return will occur *after* the tribulation—we maintain is the clear teaching of this passage. We regard the Revelation narrative as literal unless there is good reason to import symbolic meaning (and in many places there is). We anticipate a *real* tribulation, a *real* Antichrist, and a *real* return of our Lord after the tribulation with the understanding that these

80

actual events of future history are described by throughout the book.

That, in fact, is the whole point of our study—to now, before the tribulation actually begins, wh..... the rapture will follow or precede it, and then make appropriate preparations.

Predictors of doom are we? No, unless you are a reader without the hope that salvation brings. For those outside of Christ, trouble will be hot and never-ending.

One of the most cogent arguments for a posttribulation rapture and return appears in Revelation 20:5: "This is the first resurrection." That adjective *first* spells trouble for the idea that Christ will rapture the Church before the tribulation. *First*, of course, means "nothing of the same kind preceding" no matter how you turn the dictionary. And verse 4 presents the roster of saints who will participate in that first resurrection. The last part of verse 4 leaves little doubt that believers who have perished during the tribulation—"those who had not worshipped the beast or his image, and had not received the mark upon their forehead and upon their hand"—will be part of those who come to life at the first resurrection. Since no man has ever been or could ever be resurrected before dying at least once, we are forced to the conclusion that this first resurrection happens after the tribulation—after tribulation martyrs have died.

The first part of verse 4 refers to the Church of all ages. Why? Because Scripture is replete with promises that God's people will judge the nations. Paul transmits the promise to believers in I Corinthians 6:2 and II Timothy 2:12. In verse 6, those resurrected are called priests, a clear reference to the entire Church.[15] In John's record of the fifth seal (Revelation 6: 9-11), martyrs are admonished to be patient until their number is complete. Notice the parallel description of the martyrs of 6:9 and 20:4a—both killed because of the Word of God and the testimony of Jesus. Likewise, the fellow-servants of 6:11 and the tribulation martyrs of 20:4b are identical.

So Revelation 20:4 teaches that all believers are part of the *first* resurrection, which must necessarily happen after the tribulation, at the "last day," when all who believe will be raised up (John 6:40), and at the "last trump," when the dead in Christ will be raised "imperishable, and we shall be changed" (I Corinthians 15:52).

Footnotes

[15]See Revelation 1:6, where John calls himself and his contemporaries priests, and Revelation 5:9-10, where believers from every conceivable background are made priests to reign.

Scripture reading
Revelation 19:1-16, 20:1-6.

Integration
1. Review your list of verses and add to it Scripture passages which teach a two-stage rapture and return, the first happening before the tribulation.

2. If the promise of resurrection is given to those who are in Christ, should you not examine yourself in view of Scripture's teaching on man's sin and his need for a Savior? The question of your salvation is more crucial than any other proposed in this book, or anywhere else.

3. If you have asked God for forgiveness and know that His Spirit lives in you, are you ready to sing hallelujahs until the Lord returns, even if that means enduring the rigors of tribulation? Read through Revelation and notice the frequent hallelujahs, yet Christ does not return until chapter 19. How is your "waiting quotient"?

4. Consider the connection between rapture and resurrection. Throughout the New Testament, the two are used interchangeably. Since the rapture is the resurrection and, as the first resurrection, includes tribulation martyrs, where in the sequence of end-time events does the rapture occur?

5. Just as a good poem cannot be fully understood at first reading, so Biblical symbols cannot be truly appreciated with just a cursory reading. Reread chapters 19-20. Look for main characters. What do they say? What do their songs mean to

you? (Handel borrowed from Revelation 19:6 in his famous "Messiah." Listen to that selection of the oratorio in the light of Christ's return in chapters 19-20.)

Chapter Eight

WIDE ANGLE:
THE COMING OF CHRIST

In the Rest of Revelation

Between the disciple John and his Lord there was a special attachment. The Master surely groomed and nurtured each of the twelve, but John had an empathy that distinguished him from the group and upon which the Lord built an intimacy that was noticeably distinct from His relationships with the others. It was John's uncommon insight, spiritual perspicuity, and sensitive temperament that set him apart from the ordinary man. And one immortal Sunday the lone surviving disciple gazed beyond the stony shores of Patmos and saw wonders from the throne of God.

With this chapter we conclude the New Testament survey of the doctrine of the rapture. Perhaps by now you have determined that Scripture casts dubious shadows on the hope held by many Christians for a pretribulation removal. On the other hand a theory that has won the allegiance of so many sincere believers must have some scriptural support, and an impartial jury must await all the evidence. So, with trust in the same Spirit who illumined John with spiritual insight on that desolate island prison in the Aegean, let us forage through Revelation to the climax of Biblical teaching on the end times.

Revelation 1—He comes
The first reference in Revelation to the Lord's return is in 1:7,

and it states in simple yet dramatic words: "Behold, He is coming . . ."

Here is the hope of the Church, the point to which all history moves, the victory of Jesus Christ over evil and the glorification, through His victory, of His people.

Note carefully how His return is described—not secretly, but seen by every eye; not known by His people alone, but even by those who drove the spikes through His flesh; not a joyous meeting altogether, but attended with the mourning of sinners who recognize their rebellion too late. It is the same return, accompanied by the same signs Jesus set forth to His disciples in Matthew 24:29-31. Cosmic wonders will preclude His coming. Heavenly bodies will tremble in quick and irregular patterns. The people of earth will see the returning Sovereign and mourn, while the elect of God are gathered from every direction.

In 1:11, John is instructed to record what he sees in a book destined for the churches. John's scroll is to include all that he sees —those things which pertain to the past, present and future (1:19). His book, we know now, was circulated to the seven churches mentioned in chapters 2-3. That should raise a question: Since the major part of the book (chapters 4-18) describes the period of great tribulation (albeit with relevance to the tribulation of all ages), why, if the Church has nothing to do with the tribulation, was Revelation even written? Surely God's people have enough discouragement to ward off without adding more unnecessarily. A bold reading of Revelation will burrow a recurring impression that most of the book is about the tribulation. And it is addressed to the Church!

Revelation 2-3—Letters to seven churches

Three passages in chapters 2-3 are particularly applied to the rapture. Revelation 2:25-28 offers a challenge and a promise, frequent partners throughout the Bible. The clear call of the Christian is to hold fast until Jesus comes *at the end*. Those who persevere will share in Christ's authority, and to them will be given earthly rule and the "morning star"—the glorious dawning of the Savior after a dark night of cruel persecution.

Revelation 3:3 was written to Sardis, a city which twice was conquered by commandos who stole past defending sentries in the dead of night and opened the way for armies to storm the town by surprise. The warning is plain: Wake up, Christians, or fall like unprepared Sardis before Christ and His armies at His return.

To non-watchers, Christ will come as a thief in the night, but to those who are vigilant in both eyesight and activity, Christ's return will *not* come as a thief. "But you, brethren, are not in darkness, that the day should overtake you like a thief; for you are all sons of light and sons of day" (I Thessalonians 5:4). The Church will not be overtaken by the coming of the Lord as a houseowner is surprised by a robber (Matthew 24:43), but the pseudo-religionist and ego-confident moralist will not only be overtaken, but overthrown (Matthew 24:48-51).

Revelation 3:10 is a fundamental girder in the superstructure of the modern pretribulation theory. Here, it is claimed, is the *prooftext* for the removal of the Church before trouble begins. "Because you have kept the word of My perseverance, I also will keep you from the hour of testing, that hour which is about to come upon the whole world, to test those who dwell upon the earth."

The theme of escape seems apparent at the outset, but a closer look may reveal that the promise is even greater, and more applicable to Christian living, than we first imagined. In John 17:15, Jesus prayed for His people. He did not ask the Father to take them out of the world or to remove them from the scene of spiritual conflict. His prayer was that the Father would "keep them from the evil one," a phrase identical to the one in Revelation 3:10. Christ was asking for providential care and protection for His children in a world which would, under the influence of Satan, hate them. Jesus gently comforted His men in the face of impending persecution, never suggesting escape, but always encouraging them with the inexhaustible strength of God. "In the world you have tribulation, but take courage; I have overcome the world" (John 16:33).

The promise of protection for God's people is essential to the whole fabric of Scripture. Did not God preserve Noah through

86

the flood; Joseph in the court of Pharoah; Daniel among the lions; Shadrach, Meshach and Abednego in the flames of the king's hottest furnace; and Israel in Egypt during the plagues? Multiply these by the testimony of thousands of Christians who have faced persecution and imminent death, yet have been kept by God's power. This is the story of Christ's Church throughout history. Even in the death of a saint, the promise rings clear—all God's children are kept and guarded, and "not one of them perished" (John 17:12).

Because Revelation 3:10 is such an important link in our understanding of the rapture and the end times, we should not avoid a brief consideration of the original language here. One might expect that spokesmen for pre- and posttribulationism would interpret the Greek preposition, *ek (from),* in accordance with their respective theory. But the extraordinary consensus among scholars regarding this short but pivotal word leads us to a substantial and Biblically sound conclusion. Merrill Tenney writes that Revelation 3:10 is a promise to "preserve from the attack of evil rather than to remove from it by physical separation."[16] J. Barton Payne concedes that *ek* generally means *from* in the sense of *out of,* but it may mean *separated, but still in the presence of,* as it does also in John 17:15 and Galatians 1:4.[17] John Walvoord, one of the leading contemporary scholars among pretribulationists, admits that *from,* as used in Revelation 3:10, "cannot be pressed to mean absolute deliverance."[18] In the absence of any other Scripture which directly teaches a two-stage, early removal of the Church, we suggest that Revelation 3:10 is a great promise of protection through tribulation, both historically (since it was written to a church of the first century) and as the final persecution under Antichrist finds momentum.

In each of the seven letters of chapters 2-3, persecution, testing and tribulation are met by God's promise of strength to endure, and finally, when either life expires or Jesus comes, deliverance and fellowship with Him.

Revelation 4-21—Where did the Church go?
The blessed hope is the return of Christ for His Church. Our

point of issue is the time of that return. Pretribulationists claim a weighty argument for their position by the absence of the word *Church* in these middle chapters of Revelation. Since the Church is not mentioned, the conclusion is drawn that it must have been raptured.

An argument from silence is difficult to maintain. The word *Church* appears neither in I Corinthians 15, I Thessalonians 4, nor John 14. Are we to believe, then, that the truths of these passages do not apply to the Church? If so, we would be forced to edit II Timothy, Titus, I and II Peter, and I and II John from the Bible, also. The *Church* does not appear there either.

The argument from silence is difficult to apply consistently. Those who use it to support a pretrib rapture are caught in the dilemma of their own argument. Just as the Church is not explicitly mentioned in chapters 4-12, neither is the rapture. And in these chapters, the Church is not mentioned as being in heaven, either. Pretribulationists place the rapture sometime before the start of chapter 4, but nowhere is it mentioned. The only coming, resurrection, gathering and judgment described in Revelation occurs in chapter 19 after the narrative on the tribulation. Even Dr. Walvoord, who uses the argument from silence to demonstrate the Church's absence, must admit that "the rapture as a doctrine is not part of the prophetic foreview of Revelation."[19] He further concedes (rather astoundingly) that "neither posttribulationism nor pretribulationism is an explicit teaching of Scripture."[20]

Revelation 4:1-2—An implicit reference?

A voice from heaven which sounds like a trumpet speaks to John: "Come up here!" Could this be the rapture, as early removal advocates allege? It is the closest any scholar has come to finding a reference to a pretribulation rapture in Revelation. But Scripture nowhere suggests that the rapture consists of a call to heaven. The rapture is associated with the coming of the Lord more than with the going of the saints, and there is no reason given in 4:1 to associate John with the Church here. In the plain words of the Bible, John simply commences to receive a vision by ascending in the Spirit to the throne of God. Christ

Himself does not appear until the next chapter, and even then He moves not toward John or the elders, but toward the throne.

If John's reference to being "in the Spirit" is intended to symbolize the catching-up of the saints, why wait until Revelation 4:2? John is "in the Spirit" already in Revelation 1:10. (Let us hasten, not delay, the coming of the Lord.) If a counter-argument lays stress on the "door of heaven" as indication of the rapture in 4:2, we are faced with yet another obstacle. In Revelation 14:1 John perceives the Lord standing on Mount Zion, an obvious reference to an earthly scene. If John's movements in Revelation represent the future of the Church, we are due for an unexpected midtribulation return trip to earth—an unacceptable detour. The answer, we suggest, is that Revelation 4:1-2 means exactly what it says. John sees a vision.

Revelation 5:8-10—Are the elders the Church?

The Church's location after chapter 4 is said to be solved by the Authorized Version's rendering of Revelation 5:8-10, where the twenty-four elders surrounding the throne sing praise to God for their redemption—another reference, it is claimed, to the Church in heaven. Recent evangelical scholarship, however, has established that the King James translators made a miscalculation in 1611. Modern versions have corrected the passage to read in the third person. The elders say: "... for Thou wast slain, and didst purchase for God with Thy blood *men* (not *us*) from every tribe and tongue and people and nation. And Thou hast made *them* (not us) to be a kingdom and priests to our God; and they (not *us*) will reign upon the earth."

Opinion varies as to whom the elders represent, but their identification with the Church is highly suspect—they are praising God for somebody else's redemption. At best, only a tentative conclusion on their identity can be claimed from any point of view. The elders can be called heavenly beings as easily as representatives of the Old and New Covenants. The real import however of the elders' song is not lost in any ambiguity.

God has redeemed men from all nations and ethnic backgrounds—a most praiseworthy and humbling acknowledgement.

Revelation 7—144,000 evangelists?

When the disciples asked Jesus for signs of His coming, He answered by foretelling, among other things, that the Gospel would be preached to all the world (Matthew 24:14). Just as surely as His prediction will be fulfilled, there must be men to do the preaching. But who, if all born-again believers are removed by *"rapture"* before the tribulation? Here they are, say early removal theorists, the 144,000 Jewish missionaries who will carry the "Gospel of the kingdom" throughout the world, resulting in the salvation of many, despite the absence of the Holy Spirit to work the conviction that was so necessary for men to be able to respond to the "Gospel of grace."

Pretribulationists need manpower during the tribulation to effect Jesus' claim of worldwide evangelization, and the burden falls to these sealed ones of Revelation 7.

This passage has as many interpretations as there are commentators and points of view. Again, only tentative conclusions on the identity of the 144,000 are available. Some identify them as regenerate Israel, others as a Jewish remnant which will be saved at Christ's appearing, others as symbolic of the entire Church of both Old and New Testaments. Whatever their identity, one point of contention should be cleared up. John does not call them evangelists, they are not given a second great commission, and Scripture nowhere infers that they are on earth promoting a revised Gospel during the tribulation.

Jesus' claim in the Olivet Discourse must be fulfilled with the convicting work of the Holy Spirit as men preach the Gospel of salvation by grace through faith. And it must be fulfilled before He comes. For Jesus to come before the world hears would mean either a miscalculation on His part, or the importation of a quasi-gospel preached by a Spirit-less tribulation remnant.

Revelation 8-11—The seven trumpets

Revelation, as we have mentioned, is largely metaphorical.

John received visions, and used symbols and word pictures to describe them. Three major symbols comprise the main movements of chapters 4-19 and give structure to the future-history prophesied there. Each of the three symbols, the seals, trumpets and bowls, occur in a series of seven. No doubt the first four seals are most familiar, and are sometimes called the Four Horsemen of the Apocalypse. Much thought has been devoted to the timing of the three sets of symbols, whether they are concurrent, or follow each other successively, such that the seventh seal opens into the trumpets, and the seventh trumpet opens into the seven bowls, or in some sense overlap. The best approach is to regard each series as culminating at the return of Christ, and each becoming progressively more severe in extent and ferocity.

The first four trumpets are described in chapter 8, preceded by an eerie half hour of silence, and followed by a talking eagle who amplifies a message of woe throughout the earth. The fifth trumpet is the release of demonic forces to plague all who have not the seal of God on their foreheads. Their sting, unlike the scorpion they resemble, is not lethal, but brings torment. Their armament makes them indestructible and their captain is none other than Satan himself, trying desperately to win a battle he knows is already lost.

Note particularly Revelation 9:4. God deliberately restrains the satanic forces of the end time from hurting His people. Even in his final futile but vigorous attempt to overcome God's people, Satan still is subject to the sovereign authority of God, as he always has been. There is no hint that any of God's children are ever lured, browbeaten, or won over to the serpent. The redeemed have been sealed, and so escape the fate of sinners whose rebellion grows more stubborn with the increasing severity of the judgments (Revelation 10:20-21).

In Revelation 10:7, the last trumpet is about to sound the finish of the mystery of God. *Mystery* has been given many definitions, but the best suggests that the word refers to God's plan of redemption as it is revealed in the growth of the Church, His people (Ephesians 5:32). After an interlude describing the martyrdom of the two witnesses in the "great city"—a mysterious narrative itself and open to diverse interpretations—the seventh trumpet sounds. In previous studies, we found that the trump of God was to sound at the coming of the Lord and the rapture (I Thessalonians 4:16-17), at the coming of the Son of Man after the tribulation (Matthew 24:30-31), and at the resurrection and translation of the saints (I Corinthians 15:51-52). Could it be that the last trump of Paul, the trump of God, and the seventh trumpet of Revelation are all the same, and signal the same event?

Likely so, since each of the Biblical accounts uses similar language to describe the one event to which the trumpets point—the return of Christ. Power is a recurring theme in connection with the trumps. Christ comes with power at the sound of trumpets in Matthew 24:30 and Mark 13:26.

Four groups are mentioned as recipients of rewards at Christ's coming: servants, prophets, saints, and "those that fear thy name" (Revelation 11:18). Since this involves the rewarding of believers, the resurrection of the saints is strongly implied, if not demanded. Every believer of every age is included in this great roll call. Rather than four distinct groups, each phrase describes every child of God who has been faithful to His calling in obedience, witnessing, holiness and worship.

Revelation 16—The bowls of God's wrath

A problem arises in chapter 16. If the bowls are indeed the wrath of God, then all saints must have been raptured before that time—concluding that either the pretribulational rapture has a scriptural basis, or that the bowls occur after the return of Christ. A better understanding is that the bowls portray the wrath of God, but only that aspect of the wrath that is poured out on earth-dwellers, on those who have the mark of the beast, on the regime of Antichrist. This is His temporal wrath, and as such it will not fall on the believers of that period, for they will be sheltered from that wrath. The final (eternal) wrath of God, from which all believers are guaranteed exemption—eternal hell—will be poured out by God through His victorious Son at His return—and we are not appointed unto that wrath (II Thessalonians 1:7-8, I Thessalonians 5:9).

Before leaving Revelation and moving to a summary of the evidence for a *post*tribulation rapture of the Church, read through the final chapters of Revelation and breathe in the fresh and fragrant air of heaven. Paradise is the sure hope of those who can say, "Amen, Come, Lord Jesus," as John did in 22:20.

The calls to "come" in chapter 22 are the appeals of Christians throughout history for the return of their Lord. Yet in another sense, the Spirit always has called, "Come," through the preaching and witnessing of the Church (the Bride), to men who need a Savior (22:17). It is a call that no man can avoid with impunity. All who would see the beauty of heaven and sing eternal praises to the Lamb must come to Him in transparent honesty and sincere repentance. Coming to Christ, in a way, is opening a door and accepting into the home of the heart a Lord who wants to be a friend (Revelation 3:20). The door, of course, is a symbol. Pride, rebellion and indifference lock the latch, but the Lord waits. The Spirit urges, "Come."

If you are unsure of your standing before God, we suggest that you settle this most important issue without delay. Only if Christ is your present Lord will He also be your coming Redeemer. Let the Spirit's appeal sink deep within your mind and heart. Come to Christ through a prayer of repentance, a loosening of the latch; come to dinner with the Savior. "They shall hunger no more; neither thirst any more; neither shall the sun beat down on them, nor any heat; for the Lamb which is in the center of the throne shall be their shepherd, and shall guide them to springs of the water of life; and God shall wipe every tear from their eyes" (Revelation 7:16-17).

Footnotes

[16]Merrill C. Tenney, *Interpreting Revelation,* Grand Rapids: Eerdman's Publishing Co., p. 65.

[17]J. Barton Payne, *The Imminent Appearing of Christ,* Grand Rapids: Eerdman's Publishing Co., p. 78.

[18]John F. Walvoord, *The Revelation of Jesus Christ,* Chicago: Moody Press, p. 87. Dr. Walvoord, of course, concludes that Revelation 3:10 does indeed teach a pretribulation rapture of the Church.

[19]John F. Walvoord, *The Revelation of Jesus Christ,* p. 103.
[20]Walvoord, *The Rapture Question,* (1st edition), p. 148. The statement was deleted from subsequent editions.

Scripture reading
Revelation 1-21.

Integration

1. Prepare your list of verses on the pretribulation rapture for one last review. In your search through the New Testament, have you found any verse which clearly teaches the two-stage, early removal theory? Discuss your findings with the group, or ask a mature friend or pastor to assist in understanding any questions that remain.

2. If you were a member of the First Century Community Church, and were threatened by persecution and plagued by social and economic pressures because of your testimony, how would you receive a letter that claimed to describe a future period which none of you or your descendents would experience? That is what pretribulation theorists say happened. How would you react to a letter assuring you of victory in Christ? How do you react to the promises in Revelation? Do you feel that only heroes are capable of enduring tribulation, or can you say with confidence, "God will preserve me"?

3. Discuss with your study group the degree to which each could depend on the other if the Church were faced with the most intense persecution of all time. Would you stick together? How long?

4. Are you a Christian? If not, the Spirit of God calls you to Christ. Jesus said, "I will give to the one who thirsts from the spring of the water of life without cost . . . I will be his God and he will be My son" (Revelation 21:6-7). *He is coming.* Those who resist Him will beg mountains to cover them, when "the great day of their wrath has come; and who is able to stand?" (Revelation 6:16-17). Accept Him today in repentance and

faith. Ask Him to forgive you, to show Himself to you personally, to reside with you. He will, and your life will never be the same.

Chapter Nine

WHAT DOES IT ALL MEAN?

A Look at the Biblical Evidence

An old history professor at a northern Midwest university would organize his rapid-fire lectures around the idea that mankind was constantly in search of liberty, and that history was moving toward the fulfillment of that search. He claimed that no matter how gloomy the era—whether the Inquisition or Hitler's New Order—history always was moving in an upward spiral toward greater human liberty.

The prof was not a Christian, and he readily confessed to giving little thought to life beyond the grave. But he had struck on a notion that finds its strongest support in the Biblical doctrine of the Lord's return. The Bible paints a sorry picture for dreamers who foresee worldwide peace and tranquility, but a sure hope for persons who recognize their creatureliness and who repent in faith. For them, Christ is the coming Redeemer. He offers liberating strength to each person who wants to be all the person God intended persons to be. A full and balanced life is found in the footsteps of Jesus, who Himself grew mentally, physically, spiritually and socially (Luke 2:52).

Our freedom as Christians is incomplete this side of Christ's return. We are free from the guilt of sin, free from the sorrow of death, and free from the futility of working our way into God's favor. We have the Holy Spirit living in a mysterious way within us as our comforter and guide, and we know that "where the Spirit of the Lord is, there is liberty" (II Corinthians 3:17). The freedom we enjoy now is a down payment on eternity, a guarantee that makes life vital with expectancy and hope. Our freedom must be guarded, for Paul instructed us to "stand fast in the liberty wherewith Christ hath made us free" (Galatians 5:1). Yet it is incomplete.

But when Christ returns, the incomplete and partial will give way to the full and eternal. His coming is the focal point of all liberty, and without it, attempts to find liberty in the course of human history, are like trying to swim in quicksand. For a while it might be challenging, but over the long pull discouragement is bound to set in.

The return of Jesus is more than just a faddish idea; it is the fulfillment of God's promises for our redemption. We should know what the Bible says about the Lord's coming, and what the Word does not say. We should study end-times doctrine as a hope that can be put to practical use, as well as an assurance that our eternal existence in Christ is secure.

We have completed a survey of New Testament teachings[21] on the rapture and the revelation. No doubt questions still remain, and perhaps new questions have come up. Many terms and phrases have been picked up from the pages of God's Word. Lest there be confusion over their meaning, let's recap the important words and summarize the ground we have covered.

The *rapture* of the saints refers to being "caught up" in the air: the resurrection of all believers who have died since the beginning of human history and the translation of all believers who are still alive at the return. This is the *parousia* of Christ spoken of in I Thessalonians 4:15. The rapture as a Biblical doctrine always has been the hope of God's people. In recent years a change in the concept of the rapture has redefined the Lord's return into two stages, the first an early removal of those believers who have lived between Pentecost and the rapture. Pretribulationism has eliminated the signs that Jesus and Paul taught would precede the rapture, and placed them instead at the second stage of Christ's return, the posttribulation revelation in glory.

Changes in Bible teaching, whether drastic or subtle, must always be evaluated in the context of the "whole counsel of God." Our conclusion, and perhaps you share it, is that the rapture is the blessed hope of the Church, and will occur at the Lord's return after the tribulation—the only such return ever mentioned in the Bible.

The *return,* or *revelation,* is not the second phase of a two-stage appearance, but the whole and complete and "second" coming of Christ. It will be characterized by stupendous glory, cosmic upheavals, sounds of trumpets, and will include both the rapture of believers (II Thessalonians 2:1) and the wrath of God on Antichrist's regime (Revelation 19:17-21). Christians, it must be remembered, will be removed before God's final anger falls. Judgment is directed to those who have abandoned His offer of forgiveness and have set up their own perishable and powerless gods.

The return of Christ will be preceded by certain signs, among them the evangelization of all nations, the falling away of quasi-believers into a milk-toasty kind of religion, and the rise of a personal figure called Antichrist to a supremacy unprecedented in power, audacity and hatred for the truth. The return is the consummation of our hope, the goal to which The Great Commission and all other commissions are directed, the day of rest for the people of God at the climax of history (II Thessalonians 1:7). Christ will return visibly on that day, and believers will recognize Him as their Lord while Antichrist's henchmen and those who have passively accepted his leadership will realize the enormity of their compromise (II Thessalonians 2:8).

Christ will return as King and Lord to establish His sovereignty over creation in a more direct and immediate way than He has had since man fell through disobedience in the primeval garden. Jesus' coming is the fulfillment of God's plan of redemption, the morning star on the horizon of world history, the day when God's law will be vindicated and His righteousness rewoven into the fresh-spun cloth of a new world order. Far from wishful thinking, the hope for His return is grounded in the fact of Christ's resurrection. Because He was raised from the dead, we will be also. Because He has cast off the body of flesh and taken on the resurrection body, we will also. Our destiny is tied to Him, and as our life is "in Christ" now, so it will be "with Christ" then.

The *tribulation* is that period in which the conflict between Christ and evil will reach a peak in the pitched battle between the Church and Antichrist. It will be the last great heaving surge of worldly power in which the beseiged Church will appear to be headed toward inevitable extinction. Jesus described the period as trouble "such as was not since the beginning of the world" (Matthew 24:21), but added that it would be cut short by His return for the sake of the elect, His people, the Church.

We are warned to be on the alert for the rise of men who call themselves Christ. They are phonies and imposters, but their disguise will be convincing to the unwary. The book of Revelation likens the tribulation to a series of seals, trumpets and bowls in which the warnings of God are ignored for the deceptive offer of peace propagated by Antichrist and his False Prophet. Plagues, draught, economic collapse, and warfare punctuate the tribulation prophecies in Revelation, and lead to the final, culminating judgment of God, when men realize the hopelessness of their false security and the impossibility of shielding themselves from the anger of the Creator.

Many Christians have regarded Jesus' predictions of a time of trouble as a reference to the siege and destruction of Jerusalem in A.D. 70. Others have applied the prophecies in a broader sense to the persecution felt by Christians throughout the present age. To both variations we pay the respect due genuine and sincere scholarship, but withhold our approval. Surely, the tragedy of Jerusalem was a time of great trouble, and none can rightfully depreciate the sacrifice Christians have made since the faith was first preached. But we must regard these persecutions as preliminary, as terrible yet introductory, to the spoils of life and the global extent of the persecution during that coming time.

Certain Christian teachers have comforted the Church with doctrines which would remove us from the scene before the final idol is erected, in front of which men must either bow or die. To this we reply that such a hope is misleading, since Scripture not only refuses to support it, but positively discounts it in Christ's teaching that His coming follows the tribulation. Paul verifies and enlarges that theme, but nowhere offers the hope of early removal.

Too many Christians and too many churches are not preparing for the struggle of those final days.Or, should the tribulation be delayed, they are not preparing their children to prepare their children. Priorities get distorted and hope is misdirected when the idea of early removal replaces the determination to persevere in loyalty to Jesus despite the high price of discipleship. To many otherwise conscientious believers, it might be the tribulation, and not the rapture, that will come as a "thief in the night." The most urgent policy for many churches today is to apply the Coast Guard's motto to the spiritual realm—"Semper Paratus," Always Prepared.

The *Antichrist* is a person about whom enough warning cannot be broadcasted. He will rule a large part of the earth during the tribulation. He will presume to deserve the worship due only to God, and thus he derives his name. He will compact with nations and peoples but will abort his treaties to establish a totalitarianism that will make previous despots appear like benevolent bureaucrats in comparison. His claim to deity will be refused by the true Church, while the quasi-church bends in favor of survival. In retaliation for their refusal, Antichrist will drive Christians into caves and cloistered shelters, yet the truth will not be suppressed by his wild tactics. The Holy Spirit will yet multiply the proclamation of the Gospel until the day of Christ's appearing, and many will respond in faith, knowing that redemption requires bearing the Savior's cross all the way up the hill.

Again, some Christian spokesmen have treated the character of Antichrist as an allegorical personification of evil, frequently manifested in the great tyrants of history; others have identified him as a historical figure now deceased. Many pagan rulers have deserved Antichrist's name, but they are galley slaves and deck hands compared to the grand and corrupted admiralty of this Man of Sin. He must arise before Christ returns. He will fall when Christ returns. Resistance to him will be fatal to the flesh; compromise with him will be fatal to the spirit.

Our summary of Biblical truth on the Lord's return must squarely meet the arguments proposed against our conclusions. We do not claim to be seers, nor do we have all the questions answered. But our New Testament survey ought to suggest that certain pretribulational distinctives are founded on sandstone—stone in that they take the Word of God as truth, but sand in that they import theories which find support only as shadowy inferences from the Biblical text.

The two-stage return, with a rapture occurring seven years before the revelation, is not found in the Bible. Jesus speaks of His return "after the tribulation" (Matthew 24:29). Paul states that the day of Christ will not come until the falling away of the quasi-church and the rise of Antichrist (II Thessalonians 2:3-4). If the pretrib rapture is the hope of the Church, we must admit that the Church was never told about it, for not one verse or passage in the entire Bible teaches the two-stage theme. If the Church is to escape the tribulation, we must count it as an unexpected reprieve, since nowhere does Scripture lead to that conclusion. At all points, the Church is to endure until the end, and the end will be the singular and glorious appearing of Jesus Christ as Lord.

The notion that Jesus will come *for* His saints is often taught to the exclusion of the grander theme that He will be coming *with* His saints. These are not two separate comings, but one and the same. Believers alive at that time will be caught up to meet Christ in the air and proceed to accompany Him to the earth. We do not know all the logistics involved in our ascent and assumption of eternal bodies, but we do not need to know. It is enough to look for that blessed hope from the perspective of trust, faith and assurance. The pretribulational distinction between *for* His saints and *with* His saints is not proof of two returns, but evidence that when He comes, we will be with Him.

Semantic distinctions between the "day of Christ" and the "day of the Lord," and between "Church," "elect" and "saints," are not distinctions at all, but simple attempts to describe what in the final analysis lies beyond the compass of words and language—the mystery of redemption. God's children—those whom He has chosen, those who have opened the door to His indwelling presence—are the saints, the elect, and the Church. Caste systems are the inventions of selfish leaders who would avoid the humility of shared authority; they are not the lifestyle of the Church of God. In Christ perfect integration is achieved, though our life too often belies it. In Christ all barriers and divisions between people are thrown aside. All men share the common dye of sin; all redeemed men have the common presence of Christ, and all share claim to the promises of God through His Son. To divide the body of Christ is not only repugnant, but Biblically unjustifiable. An end-times theory built around those distinctions must fall with the same thud. If the redeemed of the earth are not one body in Christ, what sense has Jesus' words spoken in Gethsemane: "That they all may be one; as thou, Father, art in me, and I in thee, that they also may be one in us: that the world may believe that thou hast sent me" (John 17:21).

Three things remain in our study of the rapture. First, a survey of the history of pretribulationism with an effort to diagnose the most likely of three possible origins. Second, in chapter 11 we look at some of the thorny problems of the posttribulational approach—the problem of imminence (if Christ's return is actually scheduled for the close of the tribulation, why are we told that it is at hand?), and the Biblical reasons why the Church cannot be distinguished from the elect and the saints. And third, thoughts for the Church as it approaches God's plan for the end of the age.

Our conclusions have been drawn. The Bible has been studied. You now must decide whether our findings are Scripturally sound, for Scripture alone is profitable (II Timothy 3:16).

Footnotes

[21]You might also investigate some Old Testament references that have been associated with the rapture: Isaiah 27:12; Daniel 12:1; Hosea 11:10-11; Joel 2:32; 3:16; Zechariah 8:7; 10:9-10; 12:7.

Scripture reading

Since this chapter was a summary of our New Testament survey, you may want to backtrack and reconsider any passages that left you with questions, or simply organize more fully your conclusions. We suggest a review of the key rapture texts, with an occasional stop for memorization.

Integration

1. Complete your list, or simply discard your empty sheet, of verses that teach the rapture of the Church before the tribulation. Indirect references are not enough without some clear, unequivocal evidence for the two-stage return. Do your investigation thoroughly. Your attitude and outlook on the future is at stake.

2. Complete your comparison of what Jesus, Paul, and the other Scripture writers had to say about the second coming. Take care to note differences, and determine to resolve any apparent contradictions. The final result should fit together like cinnamon in apple pie.

3. Complete your time-chart of the end-times events. Together with your conclusions above, you should be able to locate the time of the rapture in relation to the tribulation and the return of Christ.

4. Discuss with the group your own personal journey through the study of end-times truth. Where were you at the beginning? Where are you now? Have you considered the possibility that the friends with whom you are studying and worshiping may be your companions during the tribulation? (Scary, isn't it?) Take a long look in the mirror with that same thought in mind—from their point of view.

Chapter Ten

HOW THE IDEA BEGAN

A Brief Look at History

Around the time Davy Crockett began his short career in Congress, a new idea was gaining momentum in Great Britain, an idea that won rapid popularity among evangelical Christians as a long-awaited antidote to the prevailing indifference over the Lord's promised return. It was the idea of a two-stage reentry, the early removal theory of pretribulationism.

At the time of pretribulationism's emergence, churchmen were for the most part convinced that Jesus would not come again until the world was converted. And, of course, they did not expect that for many years, even centuries. Watchfulness for the Lord's return had subsided into complacency. Even the call to preach to all nations was stymied by the anticipated longevity of the task.

Into this lazy river spurted pretribulationism with the punch of an instantaneous appearing of Christ and the awesome prospect of the Church's unannounced rapture into heaven. The spirit of the times was ready for a jolt, and the founders of pretribulationism (whoever they were) had the right diagnosis for the ailing patient, however questionable their cure.

Where did the early Church stand?

Hardly a scholar disputes the fact that the early fathers were premillennial, that they expected a personal return of Christ, and for the most part, expected Him to return soon. Their writings give evidence to a belief in a one-time, public return of Christ after a period of intense, or at least accelerating, persecution.

The *Didache*, written during the second century, warns early believers against the deception of Antichrist, and comforts the faithful with a soon-expected return of the Lord. The author leaves no doubt about a coming tribulation, claiming that there

> shall appear the deceiver of the world as a Son of God, and shall do signs and wonders and the earth shall be given over into his hands and he shall commit iniquities which have never been since the world began. Then shall the creation of mankind come to the fiery trial and many shall be offended and be lost, but they who endure in their faith shall be saved by the curse itself. And then shall appear the signs of the truth. First the sign spread out in Heaven, then the sign of the trumpet, and thirdly the resurrection of the dead: but not of all the dead, but as it was said, The Lord shall come and all his saints with him. Then shall the world see the Lord coming on the clouds of Heaven.

Other early Christian writers confirm the impression that suffering was not an extraordinary experience for the church, but a common part of Christian living. Irenaeus, the first to speak from a distinctively premillennial viewpoint, claimed that the prophecies of Antichrist, his persecution of the saints and ignominious defeat before the avenging sword of Christ, were given "in reference to the resurrection of the just, which takes place after the coming of the Antichrist, and the destruction of all nations under his rule." He places the rapture after the tribulation.

Tertullian identifies the rapture of I Thessalonians 4 with Christ's coming to destroy Antichrist and establish His kingdom. The hope of resurrection will sustain the faithful when "the beast Antichrist and his false prophet . . . wage war on the Church of God."

In the fourth century, a shift occurred. Premillennialism

suffered a major setback under the brilliant pen of Augustine, the first churchman to systematically identify the millennium with the church age. But even the amillennial point of view placed the Lord's return after the tribulation.

The early church had a view of the rapture that was definitive, reasoned, and relatively thorough. The authors must speak for themselves in the context of their time, and their writings do not present substantial support for any position other than a posttribulation rapture. Even modern pretrib scholars confess that the "advanced and detailed theology of pretribulationism is not found in the Fathers."[22] Where, then, did it come from?

Three answers have been suggested: a certain Margaret MacDonald who purportedly gave an ecstatic utterance that was the first recorded statement on the two-stage return, the Edward Irving sect which began as part of the established church but later split into an independent group, and the Darbyite movement which arose in Britain around 1830. Let us examine the evidence.

Margaret MacDonald

Dave MacPherson is a journalist who set out in 1971 to discover the roots of pretribulationism. In his brief report, *The Unbelievable Pretrib Origin,* he tells that the discovery of an obscure book by Robert Norton, a British medical doctor turned minister, proved to be the key to his search. Norton reported that a Miss M.M. "mingled prophecy and vision" to make the first distinction between the final stage of Christ's return, when all the world would see Him, and His prior appearance for those saints who watch for Him.

The circumstances surrounding Margaret's disclosure have significant bearing on her statement, as MacPherson describes them. In 1830, a revival swept Scotland that led to extreme charismatic manifestations—some no doubt genuine, and others presumably questionable. A certain James Grubb was allegedly the first "revived" person to experience any supernatural vision. When he died, his gifts fell to Mary Campbell and the MacDonald family of Port Glasgow. In the

106

spring of 1830, Margaret MacDonald received the gift of prophecy during a period of convalescence, and her unprecedented statement revealing the pretribulation rapture is said to have occurred on some evening between February 1 and April 14. Lest her revelation be questioned as the result of too much charismata, MacPherson carefully points out that April 20 (at least a week after her pretrib statement) is the first recorded instance of Margaret's experience with unknown tongues.

Before long the entire MacDonald family had experienced glossolalia, and Margaret was healed of an ailment. Her prophetic views began to spread throughout the area and reached into distant parts of Britain, carried by the enthusiastic couriers of revivalism. At some point John Darby heard about her, visited her home, and learned of the pretrib teaching. He subsequently incorporated it into his theological scheme, according to MacPherson. "Darby borrowed from her, modified her views, and then popularized them under his own name without giving her credit."

What did Margaret MacDonald say on that elusive evening in 1830? Her statement could initially be rendered as advocating pretribulationism. She certainly speaks of a *secret* rapture. The Lord's coming, Margaret asserts, will not be "something seen by the natural eye; but 'tis spiritual discernment that is needed, the eye of God in his people." Christians will see the Lord return "not with observation to the natural eye. Only those who have the light of God within them will see the sign of his appearance . . . this day shall be as the lightning to those in whom the living Christ is."

Her utterance however does not claim that the Church will escape the temptation of Antichrist. She warns Christians to watch with discernment for false christs and for the imposter Antichrist, lest they be tricked on the very eve of the Lord's return. Margaret's statement does suggest the possibility of a two-stage return, one a secret reentry for only part of the Church. MacPherson admits, in a closing footnote, that Margaret's statement at best describes a "partial rapture" of Spirit-filled saints. Perhaps, but only perhaps, the origin of pretribulationism can be found in the enigmatic M.M.

Edward Irving

Cultured despisers of pretribulationism have attempted to tie the origin of the early removal theory with the demise of Edward Irving and the alleged imbalance which invaded his parish in the form of charismatic gifts. The charge is careless, but evidence does suggest that Irving preached the germinal threads of the pretrib doctrine, however unrefined in form.

Edward Irving was born on August 4, 1772, in Scotland. He entered Edinburgh University at the age of thirteen and received a master's degree at sixteen. He was a licensed Presbyterian minister by 1815, and his oratory became well-known and respected. In 1826, he completed the translation of a monumental book—a historical oddity at the time—written by a disenchanted Catholic monk who identified the future Antichrist as the sum total of a corrupt Roman priesthood. Irving was fascinated with Manuel de Lacunza's *The Coming of Messiah in Glory and Majesty*, and it became his desire to share Lacunza's (pen name Juan Josafat Ben-Ezra) insights with English-speaking Christendom.

At the same time, Irving became intrigued with the Albury conferences, a series of prophetic meetings organized by a wealthy British banker between 1826 and 1830. He found there the excitement over end-times doctrine which postmillennialism had all but sapped from the church. By 1828, Irving's interests had expanded to include apostolic gifts. Two years later he heard that a charismatic revival had broken out in western Scotland. In 1830, Irving's prophetic journal, *Morning Watch*, drew a distinction between *epiphany* and *parousia* as representing the first and second stage of Christ's return. The Catholic Apostolic Church, which Irving founded, still teaches a split rapture with the first stage occurring before the tribulation.

The connection between tongues and pretribulationism is speculative and inferential. It should be noted that major biographies on Irving and source books on glossolalia do not mention the early removal theory in connection with tongues in his church, and there is no record that Irving himself ever spoke in tongues.

Also in 1830, Irving wrote a tract claiming that Jesus had a fallen human nature. It led to Irving's dismissal from the presbytery in 1832, and aggravated the grief that hastened his death in 1834 at the age of 42.

Scholars differ in their estimate of the man and his work. Thomas Carlyle said of Irving:

> But for him I had never known what the communion of man with man means. His was the freest, brotherliest, bravest human soul mine ever came in contact with. I call him on the whole the best man I have ever, after trial enough, found in this world or now hope to find.[23]

Nathaniel West, a respected proponent of posttrib premillennialism during the late 1800s, called Irving "erratic in some things, but still a noble soul" and applauded his premillennial views.

Did Irving originate the early removal theory? Professor Gundry thinks so, claiming that Irving "was likely the first to suggest the pretribulation rapture, or at least the seminal thought behind it."[24] Gundry cites B.W. Newton, a founding Brethrenite, as saying that Irving's attendance at Albury conferences "ruined" them by his suggestion of the secret coming. Gundry also reports on a vision received by a Robert Baxter in 1832 to the effect that Jesus would return 1,260 days from that date to rapture the saints before the appearance of Antichrist. Baxter, according to Gundry, attributed his ideas to Irving.

Iain H. Murray's *The Puritan Hope* cites Irving as the founder of the theory.

> All the salient features of Darby's scheme are to be found in Irving . . . At Albury and in Irving's London congregation a curious belief, practically unknown in earlier church history, had arisen, namely, that Christ's appearing before the millennium is to be in two stages, the first, a secret "rapture" removing the church before a "Great Tribulation" (p. 200).

S.P. Tregelles, another Brethren giant who opposed early removalism, suggests that the secret coming of Christ was first proposed around 1832.

> I am not aware that there was any definite teaching that there would be a secret rapture of the Church at a secret coming, until this was given forth as an "utterance" in Mr. Irving's church, from what was there received as being the voice of the Spirit . . . [25]

Ernest Sandeen attempts to balance the historical record. In *The Roots of Fundamentalism*, he contends that the identification of Irving or utterances in Irving's church as the source of pretribulationism

> seems to be a groundless and pernicious charge. Neither Irving nor any other member of the Albury group advocated any doctrine resembling the secret rapture . . . Since the clear intention of this charge is to discredit the doctrine by attributing its origin to fanaticism rather than Scripure, there seems little ground for giving it any credence (p. 64-65).

H.C. Whitley, in his short but sympathetic biography on Irving, neither denies Irving's early allegiance to pretribulationism nor ascribes its origin to him. He believes Irving's "apocalyptic preoccupation" gained at Albury conferences "led him most astray and overbalanced his judgment."[26] In moving prose, Whitley answers the question he poses to himself and the reader: when did the two-stage teaching dawn?

> Perhaps it was during the bitter years of his rejection in Scotland, maybe it was when, with the eyes of awareness which comes to a heart that has lost its dearest possession, he knew he must accept duty rather than love, or perhaps it was the night he lost Edward (his son), and on his lonely isle of utter desolation a door opened in heaven to disclose to his haunted and wondering gaze visions, mysteries and symbols, and the whole march of future history with the great final event to which all creation moves.[27]

Irving definitely taught an imminent return. Phrases like "our Lord draweth nigh" and "close at hand" punctuate his *Preface* to Ben-Ezra's work. But the power of his argument there is directed to an attack on postmillennialism rather than a clear statement on pretribulationism. Irving's expectation was that Jesus would return as Sovereign to gather His Church and establish His earthly reign—clearly premillennial, but not so clearly pretribulational.

In *Babylon and Infidelity Foredoomed,* Irving predicts that the first resurrection, which is to happen at the end of Antichrist's captivity of the Church, would occur no later than 1867. "The coming of the Son of Man, whereof solemn warning is given unto the churches . . . is delayed . . . till after the body of the beast shall have been destroyed, and given to the burning flame" (Vol. 1, p. 251). Apparently Irving adopted a two-stage rapture theory after 1830, since his writings before that date do not reflect it. Exit Edward Irving.

John N. Darby

Prior to the rise of the Plymouth Brethren movement and the writings of John Darby, standard premillennial doctrine held to a one-time return of Christ just before the commencement of the millennium, and just after the tribulation. Darby's radical recasting of the apocalyptic drama found enthusiastic response against the panorama of postmillennialism that prevailed in the nineteenth century. Precisely how and when Darby introduced the teaching is a matter of debate, but that he adopted it is not a question. His writings after 1830 thoroughly support the two-stage theory.

John Darby was born in London in 1800. He entered Trinity College, Dublin, at age of 14, and graduated four years later to become an Anglican priest.

Darby underwent a change in his thinking around 1830. His writings in 1829 give no mention of a secret return, and he speaks of the suffering church on earth until Christ's return. In the *Christian Herald* in 1830, he defended posttribulational premillennialism, but sometime between his writing of the article and the end of the year, reports MacPherson, Darby began to change. His division of redemptive history into "ages" and the secret rapture were introduced at a Powers-court conference around 1833.[28]

Darby taught that the tribulation was the time of Jacob's trouble, and not the business of the Gentile church. Referring to texts which deal with the tribulation, he said: "All is local and Jewish, and has no application to hopes which rest on going to meet Christ in the air."[29] He wrote pointedly and without reservation:

> We have found that the passages which speak of the tribulation first apply to the Jews on one side, and then exclude the Church from it on the other. I do not see how such a point as this could be made clearer by Scripture.[30]

Describing the rapture, Darby stated: "The great and vital truth of the rapture of the Church—I mean the *secrecy* of the rapture"[31] and later, "We go up to meet Christ in the air. Nothing clearer, then, than we are to go up to meet Him, and not await His coming to earth."[32]

Perhaps Darby foresaw the charges that later critics would turn against him. Indeed, he faced enough opposition in his own time from members of his own church. As if to fend off his detractors, he wrote:

> Let us commence by saying, that the difficulty people find in the subjects of which we are treating do not arise from the Word of God not being simple, clear, and convincing; but from this—that preconceived ideas often rob us of its natural sense. We have habits of thinking apart from the Scripture before we know it; then it is we find inconsistencies—incompatibility—in that which presents itself to us, not suspecting that this incompatibility belongs alone to human preconceived opinions.[33]

At last we find a strain in Darby to which we most heartily concur.

Assessing the patchwork
Three possible points of origin for the pretribulation rapture

are apparent from the end-times literature of the last century: Margaret MacDonald, Edward Irving, and John Darby. The first possibility is clouded by her statement, which does not clearly include a secret, two-stage return. Edward Irving is probably the originator, if indeed one individual can be credited with devising the idea. His position, as we noted, was not originally pretribulational, but he shifted soon after 1830. Irving, however, never systematized the doctrine; that job fell to Darby.

The idea was more likely conceived in its elemental form in the milieu of 1830, amid the interchange of prophetic views at the Albury and Powers-court conferences which Irving regularly attended, and matured later in Darby's teachings. The Brethren leader's swift change from historic premillennialism to pretribulationism suggests that at some point in 1830 or soon after, he began to see that the secret rapture made sense in terms of his approach to Scripture, and discovered that its inclusion in his teachings would enhance and complete his end-times doctrine.

A shadow is cast on our conclusion by two statements, both from Darby, yet irreconcilable. Noel Napoleon quotes J.N.D. as claiming that he received the teaching from no other man: "The Lord was pleased, without man's teaching, first to open my eyes on the subject."[34] Napoleon also reports that Darby once told B. W. Newton that, during a period of personal wrestling with the end-times issues, a suggestion was made to him by a Mr. Tweedy, "a spiritual man, and most devoted ex-clergyman among the Irish Brethren," which cleared up Darby's difficulty on the rapture question.[35] Another obscurity in Darby's past relates to his contact with the MacDonald family during the middle of 1830. MacPherson, we have noted, concludes that Darby plagiarized Margaret MacDonald, adapting her partial rapture statement into his own clearly two-stage teaching. At this point, only MacPherson has done pioneer research on this question, and his findings should provide a launching pad for future investigators. Whatever Darby's source, whether his own intuition or a respected acquaintance, the theory became a central theme in Brethren doctrine.

Irving, on the other hand, was a troubled man. If the idea originated in his congregation or in his associations at the British prophecy conferences, he was not to become its chief proponent. His demise after 1830 clouded the vigor of his apparently genuine intentions regarding the ministry. History has little sympathy for pronounced heretics.

The correctness of the pretribulation rapture must be weighed from Scripture, not history. Suffice it that if the theory is correct, no theologian or Christian spokesman discovered it before the events surrounding the revival movements in Great Britain around 1830. The first precise statement of the doctrine may never be found. Indeed, the idea seems to have grown with the times, coming of age in Darby's system after a shaky adolescence in Irvingism. Its begetter, in the final analysis, may be the spirit of man that begs for something new.

Footnotes

[22]John Walvoord, *The Rapture Question*, p. 52.
[23]Quoted in H.C. Whitley, *Blinded Eagle: An Introduction to the Life and Teaching of Edward Irving*, p. 34.
[24]Robert Gundry, *The Church and the Tribulation*, p. 185.
[25]S. P. Tregelles, *The Hope of Christ's Second Coming*, p. 35.
[26]H. C. Whitley, *Blinded Eagle*, p. 45.
[27]Ibid, p. 88.
[28]Cited in Ladd, *The Blessed Hope*, p. 37, and MacPherson, p. 43.
[29]*The Collected Writings of J. N. Darby*, vol. 4, edited by William Kelly, no date, p. 168.
[30]Ibid, p. 171.
[31]Ibid, p. 182.
[32]Ibid, p. 234.
[33]*Collected Writings*, vol. 1, p. 457.
[14]Noel Napoleon, *The History of the Brethren*, vol. 1, p.73.
[35]Ibid, p. 74.

Collateral reading

The most readable and thorough treatments on the history of end-times doctrine are found in *The Blessed Hope* (George E. Ladd), *The Church and the Tribulation* (Robert H.

coming imminent, that is, possible at any moment. No sign, signal, event or circumstance qualifies this coming of Christ for the church.[36]

The psychology of tension would go a long way in explaining the meaning behind Jesus' statement, "I come quickly." Let's face it, an interval of nineteen hundred and fifty years is not a "quick" return by anyone's estimate. Why then did Jesus speak in such a way? Or a better question is: How did the sovereign wisdom of His words come to be understood by some modern churchmen as meaning "maybe today," which is surely not how Peter understood Him. The disciple knew he must die. Therefore he knew that His Lord's promise to come quickly did not mean "perhaps in the next moment."

The answer, as we have suggested, lies in the whole complex of the Christian attitude and lifestyle. We are, in a sense, dead men; yet we live. We know that our highest and ultimately our only satisfaction is in knowing Christ, glorifying God, and enjoying Him forever; yet we work forty hours a week, eat with punctual regularity, and shoot for par on the links once in a while. We have the joy-giving presence of the Holy Spirit Himself within us; yet as we groan because our bodies decay, and the Spirit Himself, because He indwells us, illumines a brighter future—a fellowship unfathomable that awaits our heavenly glorification. In the same sense, Jesus instructs us to be always watchful for His return, and cloaks His teaching in the context of certain events that must happen first. True disciples live in the tension between earthly work and weariness, and the unshakable certainty of future hope. It's a healthy tension.

But psychological considerations are good only as they are consistent with the Bible, so the problem of imminency must finally be decided by Scripture. Pretribulationists have cited John 14:3 as evidence for an any-moment rapture. One of their leading scholars has written:

> The hope of the return of Christ to take the saints to heaven is presented in John 14 as an imminent hope. There is no teaching of any intervening event. The prospect of being taken to heaven at the Coming of Christ is not qualified by description of any

An examination of Jesus' strong and simple words in John 14 gives no evidence, however, for an any-moment rapture, not even in verse 3. Imminency is certainly not mentioned there. And while prerequisite signs are not part of the verse, neither is there any suggestion that His coming is any different from the one described in Matthew 24. Jesus gave the Olivet Discourse to the same group of disciples only a couple days prior to the teaching in John 14, and Matthew 24 makes it plain that He intends to come after the Antichrist and after the tribulation. Perhaps Jesus credits His disciples with enough memory-power to make a repetition of the "prior events" listed in Matthew unneccessary in John. In any case, the Lord does not eliminate the possibility of intervening events in the Gospel of John; He does fasten the disciples' foresight to the hope of *being with Him*. That's what Jesus is teaching, and that's what really matters.

Other pretribulational favorites are I Thessalonians 5:6: "Watch and be sober;" I Corinthians 1:7: "Waiting for the revelation;" and Titus 2:13: "Looking for that blessed hope, and the glorious appearing of the great God and Savior Jesus Christ." These verses allegedly support the idea that a command to *look* for the next appearance of Christ is unrealistic if that event is separated from us by great trials and persecutions which likely will decimate Christian congregations and bring much of what, in the eyes of the world, would be called destruction, devastation, and acute loss of life.

But in many matters on earth and in heaven, watchfulness is tied not to immediacy but to inevitability. We have no doubt that Jesus will return. His return, we confidently proclaim, is our blessed hope. But we are not obliged to regard it as impending simply on the basis of commands to watch for it.

Nor is it permissible to take Luke 12:40 as a prooftext that Jesus' return is imminent. "For the Son of man cometh at an hour when you think not" means, simply, that no one can pinpoint the precise time of His return. It does not speak of an "any moment" return, but of a climax to history that is beyond, indeed, above, our poor ability to predict. To forecast the hour of Jesus' return is a vain and prideful pastime. To watch for His return is a sign that our life-priorities are in proper order. Careful watchfulness is, in fact, mere obedience to the Lord's command in Matthew 6:33 to "seek first the kingdom of God."

Posttribulational opposition to an any-moment rapture is not opposition to Scripture. For example, the command to watch in I Thessalonians 5:6 is connected with the day of the Lord (5:2), which is certainly after the tribulation according to Acts 2:19-20, and after the Antichrist according to II Thessalonians 2:1-10. Even pretribulationists identify the day of the Lord as His glorious return; a passage so often cited to warn of a surprise reentry really describes the posttrib return after all.

By the same ground rules, I Corinthians 1:7 adjures us to wait for the revelation of our Lord, and the *revelation* by everybody's game plan is at the end of the tribulation. Paul tells the Corinthians, in fact, to wait for the posttribulational revelation of Christ. How then can this verse be used to teach an imminent rapture when it does not refer to a two-stage rapture, but a one-time revelation? The answer—it cannot!

In Titus 2:3, the event we are to look for is the "appearing of the glory of the great God and our Savior." Pretribulationists are committed to the viewpoint that Christ's coming in glory is a posttrib return. What they fail to see is that the Church has been commanded to wait and watch for it.

Paul puts it this way:

> Now we beseech you, brethren, by the coming of the Lord Jesus Christ, and by our gathering together unto him, that ye be not shaken in mind, or be troubled, neither by spirit nor by word, nor by letter as from us, as that day of Christ is at hand. Let no man deceive you by any means, for that day shall not come, except there come a falling away first, and that man of sin be revealed, the son of perdition" (II Thessalonians 2:1-3).

In Acts 3:21, Peter claims that heaven must receive Jesus

until the times of restitution *of all things.* Whether restitution refers to the kingdom of Israel, or the restored heavens and earth, the tribulation is the intervening event. To look for a rapture before these things are restored is like eating green apples—premature consumption can spoil one's appetite for the real thing.

Objection: But is it not proper to say that the second coming of Christ is substantially one event in two phases? The first phase is private, in that only the Church will be aware of it, and the second phase is public—visible and apparent to all men from tribulation saints to the regiments of Antichrist. For that matter, Scripture separates the Church from those saints, or elect ones, and certainly from Old Testament believers. If the Biblical term Church was meant to include saints of all ages, then it is self-evident that the Church will endure the tribulation, since Scripture assures us that "saints" will go through it. But if the "Church" applies only to a certain group of saints, namely those who have believed since Pentecost, then the Church's rapture before the tribulation becomes most probable. Posttribulationists will be sorely taxed to find tribulation saints referred to as the Church, or the Body of Christ, or as indwelt by Christ, or as subject to the rapture, or as the Bride of Christ.

Granted, if there is a special caste of Christians called the *Church,* and if the elect, the disciples, and the saints are in another league, the case is tipped in favor of the pretribulational removal.

The term *elect* certainly is used of Old Testament Israel as a nation. But Paul points out in Romans 9:6-7 that the true Israel is the Israel of faith, not of natural birth. *Elect* is used of Israel in this present generation in Romans 9:11 and 11:5,7 and 28: "Even so then at this present time also there is a remnant according to the election of grace." These believers are part of the Church also, since the Church is not segregated by race, sex, or income tax bracket, but consists of all who are redeemed in Jesus Christ.

120

Elect is used in Matthew 24 and Mark 13 to denote those men of faith who are to endure the persecution of the tribulation, and who are to be gathered together when the Lord returns after the tribulation. No doubt Jewish believers are included, but to limit the *elect* to Jews only is to drop a ball in foul territory and call it fair. Paul, in fact, calls believers in Rome *elect* (Romans 8:33), the church in Colossae is called *elect* (Colossians 3:12), and Christians in general are tagged with that label in II Timothy 2:10. Peter refers to believers scattered throughout Asia as *elect*.

Apparently Paul and Peter both used the terms *elect* and *Church* interchangeably. The Church cannot be excused from the tribulation merely because the word *elect* is used to describe believers of that crisis period.

The application of the term *disciples* to believers of the present age should be transparent at the outset. When Jesus taught His disciples, He was just as surely teaching us, too. He gave the promise of John 14:3 to the disciples. All the teachings on His indwelling presence, the Holy Spirit, salvation, and the walk of the believer, were given to the disciples. We rightfully appropriate those teachings to ourselves today.

Christ taught church-truth to the disciples in at least two specific places which refer to the end-times trouble. In Matthew 16:18, Jesus said to Peter that "upon this rock I will build My church and the gates of hell shall not prevail against it." In this church-truth, the Lord is saying that throughout history, and especially in the final persecution, the Church will stand and prevail over the gates of hell, over Satan himself. And in Matthew 28:20, the command is given to make disciples of all nations. Here is the Church's marching order until the end of the age.

So, we must believe that the Lord's instructions to the disciples are His instruction to the Church, and that His divinely perceptive and irrevocable words must not be set aside as applying only to faithful Jews.

The word *saints,* the term said to apply particularly to tribulation believers, is surely synonymous with *Church*. Paul said: To all that be in Rome beloved of God called saints"

121

(Romans 1:7) . . . "because He intercedes for the saints according to the will of God" (Romans 8:27) . . . "for God is not the author of confusion, but of peace, as in all churches of the saints" (I Corinthians 14:33). The *saints* are the Church!

Although *Church* is a different word than *saints, elect* and *disciples,* its meaning is not. Every believer is a saint, one of the elect, a disciple, and part of the Body of Christ. There are not two or three or more kinds of children in God's family—we are one in the Lord, one in the Spirit.

No evidence is available to support the notion that the Church is the Body of Christ from Pentecost to the pretrib rapture. But there are three passages which keep the Church in existence until the consummation of the age. Matthew 16 makes the Church the one prevailing institution throughout history, so that even the gates of hell, which will be most active and aggressive during the tribulation, cannot succeed in overthrowing it. And II Thessalonians 1 pictures the Church in tribulation and persecution until the revelation of the Lord Jesus "with His mighty angels in flaming fire taking vengeance on them that know not God." We also have noted that Matthew 28:20, The Great Commission, applies until the end of the age.

So, in the absence of any passage which teaches that the Church will come to the end of its journey before the tribulation, and with these three passages which teach that the Church will continue until the consummation of the age, we must conclude that the claim of two-stage removalists—that the Church is a special group of God's people subject to a pretribulation rapture—is unsubstantiated. In fact, the charge of pretribulationists that "the whole point of posttribulationism would be conclusively won by just one reference placing the Church in the tribulation"[38] has been straightforwardly answered. II Thessalonians 1:7 teaches just that!

Objection: But one profound difficulty must not, nay, cannot be overlooked. The return as foretold by Christ, and the rapture of the Church as described by Paul, are different enough to suggest that each is referring to different events. Not

122

that either is in competition or contradiction, but that in the holy plan of God for the revealing of truth to men, He deemed it wise to transmit a clear message of the rapture through the Apostle. Thus we find in the New Testament epistles a body of end-times truth that had not received prior utterance in so explicit a fashion.

Are they really so different? Both the Gospels and the epistles predict that the coming of Christ will be preceded by terrible evil (Matthew 24:12; II Thessalonians 2:7), false christs (Matthew 24:5,24; II Thessalonians 2:4), Antichrist in the temple (Matthew 24:15; II Thessalonians 2:4), false security (Matthew 24:37-51; I Thessalonians 5:3), danger of sleep (Matthew 25:5; Romans 13:11-12), and birth pangs (Matthew 24:19; I Thessalonians 5:3).

And the coming of Christ will be in triumph (Matthew 24:27-31; II Thessalonians 2:8), power (Matthew 24:30; II Peter 1:16), great glory (Matthew 24:30; II Thessalonians 1:9), release from trial (Luke 21:28; II Thessalonians 1:7), sudden destruction (Matthew 24:39; I Thessalonians 5:3), universal judgment (Matthew 25:31; Romans 2:8,9,16), and will announce the reign of Christ (Matthew 25:31; II Timothy 4:1). Both Christ's words and the Apostle's appear as identical teachings in the Gospels and the epistles.[39]

Objection: But who will populate the Millennial Reign if all believers are to be resurrected and translated at a posttrib return, and all the ungodly are to be judged with the sword? Where do millennial inhabitants come from?

This is a "yes, but" question similar to so many that are lodged against Biblical truth. It's the kind of question that draws its ammunition from the untold, or partially told, portions of God's truth. Answers to "yes, but" questions depend on inferences from the Biblical evidence, or on some occasions, on a simple "I don't know, God has not told us."

However, Zechariah speaks to that question in Chapter 14:16: "And it shall come to pass *that every one that is left,* of all the nations which came against Jerusalem shall even go up from year to year to worship the King, the Lord of hosts . . ." Evidently certain peoples of the world will survive the second coming judgment, since they will have been relatively untouched by Antichrist. When we say that Antichrist will be a world ruler, we cannot necessarily mean that he will rule every tribe on every continent. The term *world ruler* is not necessarily all inclusive.

In Luke 2:1, the beloved physician relates that just prior to the birth of the Messiah, a decree was given by Caesar Augustus that "all the world should be taxed." Did every man living at every point of the globe return to his home town for the tax levy? Certainly not. The phrase "all the world" had a limited meaning, namely, the context of the Roman empire. Luke intended no more than that.

In the same way, the world ruler Antichrist will govern and control a vast portion of the world; economic systems and modern weaponry will be under his visage. But certain pockets of the world's population may not directly feel his sting, and so might be spared the judgment. It is over these people that the Lord shall "rule with a rod of iron" (Revelation 2:27).

Two other groups appear to qualify for entering the millennial kingdom in natural bodies. In Revelation 14:1 the 144,000 sealed ones of Israel are shown standing with Christ on Mount Zion, evidently having survived the tribulation to reign with their Messiah. And all those Israelites who see Christ returning in power and glory, and who claim Him as their Messiah, will be gathered together in Israel to rule with Christ (Jeremiah 32:37-40; Jeremiah 33:14-16; Zechariah 12:10; 13:9; and Romans 11:26).

Other answers also could be given. It is not neccesary. The certain truth of Scripture teaches that Christ will return once; all the why's and how's and unanswered questions will have to await that time for their resolution.

Footnotes

[36]Herman A. Hoyt, *The End Times* (Chicago: Moody Press, 1969), p. 97.
[37]John Walvoord, *The Rapture Question*, pp. 78-79.
[38]John Walvoord, *The Rapture Question*, p. 145.

[39]For a complete comparative analysis of end-times doctrine in the Gospels and the Epistles, see Alexander Reese, *The Approaching Advent of Christ,* (London: Marshall, Morgan and Scott, Ltd), pp. 259-261.

Scripture reading

Review the passages cited in this chapter.

Integration

It's time for a final exam on the material we have covered in our study. Of the two alternatives, one is Biblically sound, the other is not. From your study, determine where the following pretribulational statements find their Biblical support.

1. The rapture will occur *before* the tribulation. _____
_____

2. The rapture will occur at least 7 years before the return of Christ. _____

3. The rapture is the next event on God's prophetic calendar._____

4. The rapture is for the Church; the return is for the saints, the elect._____

5. The rapture will be secret._____

6. The rapture may take place "at any moment." _____

7. The rapture will surprise Christians as a thief in the night._____

8. The rapture is, and always has been, imminent. _____

9. The rapture is different from the coming of the Lord. _____

10. The rapture is the blessed hope of the Church. _____

11. Christ comes only "to the air" at the rapture. _____

12. Christ and the Church return to heaven after the rapture. _____

13. No prophecy will be fulfilled before the rapture. _____

14. We are to look for, watch for, and be ready only for the rapture._____

125

15. There are *two* comings of Christ, distinctly different, yet future._____

16. There are *two* resurrections of the righteous, different, yet future._____

17. There are *two* last trumpets, distinctly different, yet future. _____

18. The Holy Spirit will be taken out of the world *before* the tribulation._____

19. The Church will be taken out of the world *before* the tribulation._____

20. The translation of the living saints occurs *before* the tribulation. _____

21. The resurrection of the righteous occurs *before* the tribulation._____

22. The day of Christ is different from the day of the Lord. _____

23. Rewards are to be given out in heaven during the tribulation._____

24. The judgment seat of Christ is in heaven during the tribulation. _____

25. The Marriage of the Lamb takes place in heaven during the tribulation._____

26. Christ will come once before He comes to destroy the Man of Sin._____

27. The Church will *not* go through the tribulation. _____

28. There are to be 144,000 Jewish evangelists in the tribulation._____

29. A different gospel will be preached during the tribulation._____

30. The tribulation is the wrath of God._____

31. God will not resume his work with Israel until He has finished with the Church._____

Does the Scripture teach one return or two? Before the tribulation or after? A glorious return or secret? Do your answers to these questions make any difference in how you live, how you relate to your local church, how you discipline your Bible study and prayer, how you yourself do the work of making disciples?

Chapter Twelve

POSTSCRIPTS FOR THE CHURCH

In Light of the Lord's Return

Armies do not prepare for battle by anticipating retreat, and Christians will find no tribulation strategy in plotting their early removal. Positive steps are the call of the day, not just to protect our flanks from the encroachment of Antichrist's rangers, but to revitalize the proclamation of the Gospel, and to recover the vigor of working in great cities and continents that once were considered evangelized, but have quietly slipped from the fold.

How can the Church prepare herself for tribulation? By adopting the Spirit-filled attitudes and priorities that were intended always to characterize her. The Bible contains no classified instructions labelled "Open Only in Case of Tribulation." It simply presents a life of constant discipleship that is ready to shoulder the world's rejection whenever it appears—and it will!

The Church and imminency

Jesus is coming soon. This has ever been the end-times message of the Church, and it should be so today. His approaching return is a sure incentive to pure and sacrificial living by the saints of God, and a stern warning to those who put off repentance for a crisis day. Jesus' coming, perhaps scheduled for this generation, cannot happen until the final great persecution of the Church. But this does not dim our eye with fear or cloud our hope for salvation.

The return of Christ is imminent in the sense of its potential nearness, but closer still is the tribulation which must precede it—sobering thoughts for a soft church.

> Let us suppose that we are in fact in the very last days, and within a matter of months or a few years at most, God moves upon the events of world history so that suddenly a new Caesar or Mussolini or Hitler or Stalin appears who is unquestionably the Antichrist. Suppose that he . . . demands a worship of himself and his state upon penalty of death. Suppose that martyrs begin to fall by the hundreds of thousands. Suppose that suddenly the people of God find themselves engulfed in a horrible persecution at the hands of the Antichrist when they had been assured repeatedly on the authority of the Word of God that this experience would never befall them. What would be the result?[40]

Moreover, if the Word of God clearly teaches that Christians will be on the earth during the tribulation, and does not teach a phase-one early removal, then we who see it have a responsibility to prepare the Church for whatever may come, even though in many circles this unwelcome message will receive a hostile reception.

The Church and missions

Christians are ambassadors, messengers, bearers of good news, communicators of the atonement achieved by Jesus Christ for the restoration of fellowship between God and His creatures that was aborted in Adam's sin. Mark 13:10 and Matthew 24:14 make it clear that God's program for the Church is *first* the worldwide preaching of the Gospel, and *then* the end. First the Church completes the task assigned by Jesus at His ascension and then He will come again. In Revelation 7:7, a word-picture of God's throne at the time of the end, people are present from "all nations, kindreds and tongues"—evidence that all the world will hear, and some from every nation will be among the redeemed. This has been the motivating force behind missionary work throughout the

128

Church's history, and will be until the Lord signals that the final day has come.

Peter instructs in his second epistle that the Church is to be "looking for and hastening the coming of the day of God" (3:12). Is he actually saying that Christians can speed up God's plan for the world? God is in charge of keeping time, but the unavoidable lesson is that Jesus will wait until the world has heard, and our efforts to finish the job mean that the Lord's own qualifications on His return will be met all the sooner. What, then, delays Christ's appearing? The timing of a sovereign God and the responsibility of a commissioned Church. For our part, we can see the job complete if Christians would rally to the cause of home and foreign missions, using all the strategic equipment of mass communication and all the personal opportunities of everyday conversation. Christ will not return until every tribe and nation is evangelized. The Church has been commissioned to evangelize. The sooner the Church does it, the sooner the Lord may return.

The Church and Antichrist

Since the Church is to undergo the tribulation, we would do well to know the Bible passages which describe the Man of Sin. We will need both to recognize and resist him. Although some "prophecy experts" have pointed an accusing and premature finger at contemporary diplomats and world leaders, there will come a time when the whole Church of God will be able to point to Antichrist, for he will be revealed with unmistakable clarity.

He will bring peace to Israel through a negotiated treaty, but will break the agreement after a brief coexistence and demand that their national worship cease (Daniel 9:27). He will rise as the undisputed leader over a federation of ten Western nations, taking over three of them and gaining the allegiance of the other seven (Daniel 7:24). He shall extend his rule over the entire globe and ultimately tread it down and break it in pieces (Daniel 7:23). He will blaspheme God (Daniel 7:35). He will gain worldwide fame through recovery from a mortal wound (Revelation 13:3), and his power will be turned against the saints in particular and the world in general (Revelation 13:7). His subjects will be given a brand on their hand or forehead, without which no one will be able to buy or sell (Revelation 13:16-17). He will oppose God, and will infatuate himself as above God. He will demonstrate his claim to deity by assuming God's place in the temple at Jerusalem (II Thessalonians 2:4). He will deny that Jesus Christ is come in the flesh—the specific mark of the deceiver and the Antichrist (II John 7).

Christians must be ready to identify and renounce him, for those who accept his leadership by receiving the brand will "drink of the wine of the wrath of God . . . and shall be tormented with fire and brimstone" (Revelation 14:9-11). Though martyrdom will be widespread, many believers will survive the ordeal and witness the coming of the Lord (I Thessalonians 4:16).

The beast is identified by the number 666, but scholars differ on how that should be applied. Perhaps it will be the numerical value of Antichrist's surname, or maybe it is a symbol for man's rebellious urge to be his own god—an urge brought to its blasphemous peak in the person of Antichrist. But his most prominent identifying mark will be that pseudo-resurrection miracle of coming to life after receiving the mortal "wound of death."

The book of Revelation gives timely instructions on how to face persecution with the right attitudes. We are to endure with patience, because "he that kills with the sword must be killed with the sword" (13:10). We are to keep the commandments of God and the faith of Jesus (14:13). We are not to love our lives more than death (12:11), but to anticipate heaven rather than long to remain on earth (7:14-17), and to be faithful unto death so as to wear the crown of life (2:10).

Peter conveys God's instructions to rejoice in the light of our living hope, our incorruptible inheritance reserved in heaven, our salvation ready to be revealed in the last time. No matter how difficult the trials, fire-hardened faith will be "found unto praise and honor and glory at the appearing of Jesus Christ" (I Peter 1:3-7).

Our attitude should be a reflection of our Lord, "who, for the joy that was set before him, endured the cross, despising the shame, and is set down at the right hand of the throne of God" (Hebrews 12:2).

The Church and prophecy

The evangelization of the world is the primary and arresting task of the Church, but not to the exclusion of all other pursuits. The study of prophecy is just one of the many capillaries that feed balance, health and vigor into the spirit of a Christian. Too often Christians become obsessed with prophetical paperbacks to the point of neglecting serious study of the Bible itself. The book of Revelation begins with a promise of blessing to all who read and hear of future events, and all of us should be intelligently informed through direct Bible study to look for "that blessed hope and appearing of the glory of the great God and our Savior Jesus Christ" (Titus 2:13).

In all this, our attitude must be one of watchfulness, primarily in the conduct of our daily lives in light of the Lord's coming, and secondarily watching for the event itself with its attendant historical crosscurrents.

The Church and itself

The single most devisive element in the Church is the people who worship there. If only the serene and reverent beauty of the arches and altars could be left alone, if the people would stay home, such unity would prevail in the sanctuary. Or, when they did come, if silence could be enforced. Difficulty, division and squabbling would cease if the Christians stopped talking to each other.

Yet, most churches are made up of people, and they most often talk together as well. But conversation, to our shame, too quickly becomes controversy, and the area of end-times events is no exception. In some circles deviance from pretribulationism has been reckoned as the first glowing embers of apostasy. The story of one young man, now a leading Bible scholar, who was intent on foreign service but was refused acceptance by a fundamental mission board because of

131

posttribulational leanings, is not uncommon. Less spectacular but equally devastating are the untold stories of ostracism and exile because a Christian took Christ's Olivet Discourse to mean what it says.

We submit that a proper and Biblical view of the end times is extremely important, but should not be the basis for fellowship or cooperation. Nothing short of an attack on the person of Christ Himself or His revelation in the Word should touch the warning bell on our acceptance alarms. When secondary doctrines become the central issues of cohesion or cleavage within the Church, then the Church has spent too much time within itself and needs to get out, to feed the hungry and clothe the stranger, to forget internal differences, and to rechannel energy* into evangelism until the task becomes such an overwhelming passion that intramural fastidiousness seems boring, even profane, in comparison. Regarding end-times doctrine, unity must be grounded in the belief that Christ will return in person, and in our common commitment to be about His business *until.*

When tribulation comes, unity will become a most precious commodity for God's tribulation people, and unity is possible only when we corporately fix our eyes on the One who, just before His own tribulation, prayed on our behalf: "I do not ask Thee to take them out of the world, but to keep them from the evil one" (John 17:15).

Footnotes
40George E. Ladd, *The Blessed Hope*, p. 159.

Scripture reading
Acquaint yourself with the promises of God in Scripture. Take heart from them, and learn them.

Joshua 1:9; Psalm 16:11; Psalm 27:1; Psalm 107:9; Proverbs 3:25-26; Isaiah 12:2; Isaiah 26:3; Isaiah 58:10-11; II Timothy 1:7; and many, many more.

Integration

1. Evaluate your own priorities—financially, recreationally and vocationally. How many wasted hours could be employed to show Christian friendship to a neighbor? How much of your time is lost in unproductive indulgence? How susceptible are you to unnecessary wants created by constant exposure to advertising, and how much of the cash spent on those wants could be redirected to needy Christians and evangelistic programs? For an accurate picture, don't take your own evaluation—ask a friend.

2. Does your concept of Christian unity extend to believers in your denomination, your political party, your country, your race, or your world? It's a serious question. Too few of us break out of the cloister into the true unity of the Body of Christ. Our little corner is more comfortable (and maybe more righteous).

3. Indulge in some practical planning with your Bible study group. How will the tribulation change the lifestyle of your church? Are you prepared for house churches, night prayer meetings in basements with shades drawn, economic deprivation and cooperation, extreme inflation, cataclysmic catastrophies, imprisonment, mass trials? Will you open your home or apartment as a hiding place for accused brothers? Will you train your children in the courage of standing alone? Will you love Christ, and be loyal to Him, above all?

4. Practical hints for spiritual exercise now: (a) Take up a campaign of Scripture memory with a friend, a wife, or both. Two makes it easier. (b) Try fasting. Donate the cost of the meal to a mission involved in alleviating world hunger. It's not unspiritual to give of your plenty to supply another's needs. And it might give you and your family firsthand experience with the pangs most world citizens feel as a steady diet. (c) Get involved in an evangelism program. If you feel inept and inadequate, find or organize a training program. If your church has one, get into it. Time is God's gift. Someday He will ask how you used it, and you'd better have more to show than expertise in TV reruns. (d) Develop a daily Bible study and prayer time. Spiritual growth results when time is spent with

God. Eternity will be spent with Him—learn to enjoy His presence now. (e) Begin to spread the Word—the King is coming! Christ will return. Christians must prepare; sinners must repent. Eternity is closing in. Be strong, endure. Even so, come, Lord Jesus (Revelation 22:20).

BOOKS FOR FURTHER STUDY

The following list of books and pamphlets is not a complete guide for the student of the end times, but it will start you searching. Two books are essential for your library and for a deeper sweep of the evidence for a posttribulational rapture:

Gundry, Robert H. *The Church and the Tribulation* (Zondervan, 1973). Professor Gundry has accumulated strong linguistic and comparative Biblical evidence to prove his case for the posttrib rapture. His book is concise and readable, both for the serious student and the interested layman.

Ladd, George E. *The Blessed Hope* (Eerdmans, 1956). The dean of posttribulationists sums up the Biblical alternative in this classic book. An excellent section on the history of rapture teaching is a highlight of this one.

THE CASE FOR POSTTRIBULATIONISM

Birkey, Del. *The Biblical Basis for the Post-Tribulation Rapture* (His Community Church, Elmhurst, Ill.) A mimeo graphed survey of relevant New Testament passages with supporting arguments. Price one dollar.

Douty, Norman F. *Has Christ's Return Two Stages?* (Pageant Press, 1956). A short classic with a concluding plea for toleration.

Katterjohn, Arthur D. *The Rapture—When?* (220 East

135

Union, Wheaton, Illinois 60187). A comprehensive booklet examining every prophetic New Testament Scripture suitable for personal study or group discussion. Price one dollar.

MacPherson, Dave. *The Late Great Pretrib Rapture* (Heart of America Bible Society, 1974). An outspoken author attacks the writings of the pretrib rapture theory and exposes their contradictions, false claims, and misuse of Scripture.

Payne, J. Barton. *Encyclopedia of Biblical Prophecy* (New York: Harper & Row, 1973). If you have a question on what the Bible says about the end times, this book has the answer.

Payne, J. Barton. *The Imminent Appearing of Christ* (Eerdmans, 1962). A non-traditional approach reconciling the posttrib return with "any-moment" imminency.

Reese, Alexander. *The Approaching Advent of Christ* (Marshall, Morgan & Scott, Ltd., 1937). A strong critique of "Darbyism" which was the standard posttrib defense of a preceding generation.

Tregelles, S.P. *The Hope of Christ's Second Coming* (Sovereign Grace Advent Testimony, 1886). This early Brethren leader states the case of those who could not follow Darby's end-times theory. The book is available in a recent paperback issue.

THE CASE FOR PRETRIBULATIONISM

English, E. Schuyler. *Re-Thinking the Rapture* (Southern Bible Book, 1954). Moderate pretribulational.

Pentecost, Dwight. *Things to Come* (Dunham, 1958). A full defense of modern dispensationalism.

Stanton, Gerald B. *Kept from the Hour* (Zondervan, 1956). Arguments for pretribulationism based on Revelation 3:10.

Walvoord, John F. *The Rapture Question* (Dunham, 1957). The strongest presentation. Note the 50 arguments for pretribulationism.

Wood, Leon. *Is the Rapture Next?* (Zondervan, 1956). He still thinks so.

THE HISTORY OF PRETRIBULATIONISM

Irving, Edward, "Preliminary Discourse" to *The Coming of*

Messiah in Glory and Majesty, by Juan Josafat Ben-Ezra (L.B. Seeley, 1827). A book-length exposition by one of the pretrib founders.

MacPherson, Dave. *The Unbelievable Pretrib Origin* (Heart of America Bible Society, 1973). The first pretrib statement is traced to a Scottish lass in 1830.

Noel Napoleon. *The History of the Brethren,* vol. 1 (W.F. Knapp, 1936). A reliable reference on Darby's views.

The Collected Writings of J.N. Darby, vol. 4, William Kelly, ed. (Morrish, no date). The words of the leader himself.

Whitley, H.C. *Blinded Eagle: An Introduction to the Life and Teaching of Edward Irving* (Alec R. Allenson, Inc., 1955). A sympathetic treatment of a man who went astray.

GENERAL SURVEYS

Ladd, George E. *Commentary on Revelation* (Eerdmans, 1972). The book of Revelation explained from the posttribulational point of view.

McMillen, S.I. *Discern These Times* (Revell, 1971). A stimulating commentary on Revelation suggesting that contemporary events fulfill many of the Apocalyptical scenes. Complete with diagrams and a study guide.

Tenney, Merrill C. *Interpreting Revelation* (Eerdmans, 1957). A topical commentary on the book of Revelation, but its scope goes far beyond that. Most helpful, and fair to all sides.

SHARE THE WEALTH
WITH YOUR FRIENDS
WITH LOW COST
NEW LEAF LIBRARY BOOKS

The Wonderful Way of Living

Christian Life